Bravado Brothers

Bravado Brothers

By

Ildefonso Soto Jr

Author's Note

Inspired by the countless movies I have watched throughout the years involving organized crime, and having grown up in an environment where many of these folks were my neighbors (wink, wink) in Brooklyn, N.Y., I can honestly say, without preconception or stereotype, that this particular genre, especially on a cinematic level, is one of my favorites. Without any question, this was one of the most entertaining writings I have ever created.

All the characters and sequence of events written in this book are fictional and by no means represent or attest to actual crimes or testimonies. Bravado Brothers, in essence, is a synthesis of multiculturalism, yesterday meets tomorrow, and comedic dark humor I am certain many will find entertaining or discriminative in nature; a win-win in my opinion.

As you read along and become infused with the humorous storyline, you will notice character formulations that are unusual and unorthodox to persons or fans familiar with this particular genre. Instead, this novel was created and designed in order to avoid replicating character clichés and events; it exists to introduce a diverse perception of a world so many of us know so little about.

Bravado Brothers is my third complete novel, and I am truly grateful for not just rising from the ashes from the dishonest folks that preyed on my ignorance in this industry, but also sincerely grateful that God has presented me with a great group of folks who pride themselves on their talents—they are as follows:

Line editor, Kate Weimer (found on your browser at www.almostenchanted.com/ and on Twitter @kateweimer90). Thank you for your patience and, most importantly, thank you for your level of passion for what you do. You are a true professional!

D.L. Maffett, Sr. (www.tacticalpencil.com): Creator, Artist and Author of the soul of a hero, and designer to the Bravado Brothers cover art and my other books. You are a good friend, blessed with raw talent and passion for what you do. I offer my thanks.

To my parents, who I admire and love so much. They have gone through a lot in life together. They began with very little, and have gained a wealth of appreciation for the rights-and-wrongs they have been bestowed in life. As I look at them grow old with time, I can see that, despite their challenges, they are at peace with their maker. Thank you for opening my eyes and reminding me that life is too short, and to accomplish our dreams and passions is just as important as the air we breathe and to cherish every moment as if it were my last. Gracias, Mami y Papi.

Bravado Brothers

To the beautiful woman in my life, my soulmate, my wife. Admittedly, I have some serious issues I have yet to overcome, and somehow-someway, beyond my intolerable behavior often too difficult to decipher, I thank you for loving me unconditionally, standing by my side, and being my passenger on this joyful journey God has granted me. You have kept me balanced!

To my mini-tribe of children that I truly love and cherish, who helps in keeping life's perception clear. Dad loves you all.

It is without debate, that along with my wealth in love, gratitude, and my family, there is a higher life force that is unconditionally and always looking out for my best interest, therefore with that acknowledgement, I wish to give thanks and praise to my Lord and Savior Jesus Christ.

Never have I ever experienced glorious moments in life, or hard hardships for that matter, that I have never thanked him for. He is without question the center of my universe and as I have mentioned in my previous writings, I thank my creator for allowing me to repeatedly fall, and fall hard! For if it wasn't for my stumbles and hardships, standing upright would prove to be difficult.

Thank you GOD for picking me up, dusting me off, and sending me on my way!

Gratias autem Deo,

Salute

-Ildefonso

Chapters

I.	Blind Fate	1
II.	A Deadly Ass Chewing	35
III.	Dodging Heiman	46
IV.	Just A Few Things	58
V.	Venomous	71
VI.	Clinton	79
VII.	Pig's Eye Landing	92
VIII.	Reputation Is Everything	104
IX.	A Chihuahua Against a Pit Bull	111
X.	Brooklyn Park	122
XI.	Czech'd	140
XII.	Mouth Full Of Metal	145
XIII.	What A Way To Go	152
XIV.	A Casino in the Rough	170
XV.	Panting From The Skirmish	185
XVI.	Out Of Towners	194
XVII.	Truth Is Like a Double Edge Sword	214
XVIII.	Before Me, Was We	227
XIX.	Third Wheel	236
XX.	By Virtue Of	260
XXI.	Mistaken Identity	276
XXII.	Goodbye For Now	295

Bravado Brothers

Chapter I

Blind Fate

"I hate when you do stupid shit like this. All you are doing is wasting time. Get this fucking over with already and let's get the hell out of here Fabian. We're gonna be late."

"Frankie, do I ever disturb you in any way when you are doing your thing?"

Bravado Brothers

"You're shitting me, right? You're always fucking with me when I'm trying to get my shit done. Why am I even discussing this with you? Just hurry the hell up Fabian."

"Just one minute, I'm almost there."

"Screw this, I have to go to the bathroom. I hope you're done when I get out because not only is your brother waiting outside for us, but he is going to lose his mind and blow our cover by coming up here and fucking everything up."

"Frankie, I thought you just said you were going to the bathroom? Get the fuck out of here already and let me finish this. It's not as easy as you think."

"Fabian, all that shit you're doing is pointless!" Frankie replied as he slammed the bathroom door behind him.

"Alright, I'm almost done here," Fabian whispered to himself as he stared into a mirror he was holding above his shoulder while trying to focus on his line of sight from his pistol.

"Almost there."

"Hey, what the hell is taking you guys so long?" Sebastian, Fabian's older brother asked as he cautiously opened the entrance door.

The unexpected entrance, which caught Fabian by surprise, caused him to prematurely squeeze his trigger and miss his target.

"What the fuck, you're not done yet? I thought you guys would be walking down the stairs by now," Sebastian said with a puzzled look.

"Well that's just fucking great, you made me miss," Fabian angrily responded.

"Where's Frankie?"

"He's in the shitter!"

"What the fuck? What are you yelling at me for?" Sebastian shouted back as he looked around the apartment.

"Because you never knock. As always, you barge in."

"What do you mean I always barge in? Since when do I always barge in?"

"Well you do and now I have to start all over again."

"What do you mean you have to start all over again? And point that shit somewhere else before I point mine at you to see if you like it!"

"Sebastian I'm not in the mood to argue with you. Step the fuck aside so that I can finish this."

"Ahh guys, I'm sorry to intervene in your sibling conundrum, but our target just jumped out the window," said Frankie drying his hands.

As the distinctive sound of a body landing on top of a car, and the subsequent blaring car alarm caught their attention, Fabian and Sebastian, who briefly looked at each other in disbelief, remained silent and still.

"Why didn't you tie the fucking guy up? Sebastian asked as he cautiously walked toward the window and peeped his head out.

"I did, but he must have loosened the knot. I don't know how he got out of it, to be honest," replied Fabian with a questionable look.

"Did you tie his legs up?"

"I…I…I think I did."

"Fabian, please don't tell me you were trying to shoot him with your back facing him, and aiming your gun while looking at the mirror," Sebastian said, as he thought back to a few days ago when they watched a Western and a character tried to accomplish that very act.

"Oh shit. That motherfucker is laid out on top of a car, still strapped to the chair."

"Frankie, whose car?" Sebastian concernedly asked.

"Well, it's safe to say it's not your old man's ride, but the strapped-up fucker did land on the car next to it which is not a good thing, especially when we have to get out of here."

"Fuck, my ragtop is down."

"Yeah...yeah it is," Frankie responded, looking out the window.

"Is there any blood splatter?"

"Well Sebastian, it's really hard to tell since we are about eight stories up and it's kind of dark."

"You stupid motherfucker. You couldn't just shoot the cocksucker right away, you had to toy with the son-of-a-bitch for your fucking amusement."

"Sebastian, don't start cursing at me and expect me to stay quiet."

"No you stupid-fuck. I should just shoot you right here myself!" Sebastian angrily shouted, pulling out his gun on his kid brother.

"Will you guys chill the fuck out?" Frankie intervened. "We need to figure out how we are going to get out of here undetected. In a couple of minutes CPD is going to be here, and I don't know about you, but if I were them, I'm not going to assume flyboy decided to jump out the window. As a matter of fact, it was one of those Sillitoe Tartan hat wearing motherfuckers, I'm going to assume captain carboy was thrown out from this very building; but that's just me."

"Why wouldn't they believe that he jumped?" Fabian asked with a serious face.

"You're fucking kidding me right?" Frankie responded as he looked at Fabian perplexed.

"Listen, I can hear the sirens," Sebastian said, silencing them. "Let's all go to the roof, cross over several buildings to the opposite side of the block, head to the pizzeria just a few blocks away, order a pie, and walk back towards the car, and act like what the fuck just happened before driving off."

"Sebastian, I'm not challenging your idea—as a matter of fact, it's a pretty good one—but, are you fucking crazy?" Frankie asked.

"Frankie, that's my old man's car, and there is no way on Earth I'm abandoning it at a crime scene so that it can be surrounded by cops and paramedic's, and taped off with yellow crime scene tape."

"Then why don't you move it yourself?" Fabian asked.

"Fabian, if I were you, I would shut the fuck up right about now."

"Go ahead and threaten me one more time."

"You guys need to chill the fuck out, and let's start working on our crazy escape plan," Frankie said to the two brothers who were staring confrontationally at each other as he cracked open the front door to check the hallway.

"Alright, it's clear. Let's go."

"If there is blood, glass or anything out of place in Dad's car, because you were too busy demonstrating to yourself a useless trick to yourself, I will never forgive you," Sebastian said to Fabian, psychologically preparing himself to what the car might look like.

"Shut the hell up about that car, and let's focus on not being caught by anyone. If memory serves me correct, plenty of people saw us park at that very spot, and enter the building. Not to mention, you were standing in front of the building like Enzo the Baker for some time, before you decided to enter the apartment and fucked up my shot."

"I fucked up your shot? Me?" Sebastian questioned him as they ran out of the apartment and up the stairs.

"Yeah, you. I had everything under control before you came in. Ain't that right, Frankie?"

"Fabian don't get me involved."

"What does that mean?"

"It means don't get me involved in this shit," Frankie responded as he approached the roof door.

"So what you're saying is that I didn't have anything under control?" Fabian asked him, breathing heavy.

"Fabian, I was telling you for over five minutes to shoot the motherfucker, and all you were doing was staring at yourself in the mirror."

"I was trying to focus, you half-spic, half-polack motherfucker."

"Look, I really don't give a fuck whether you were trying to impress me or yourself, but right now we have a serious fucking problem," Frankie said.

"And what's that?" Fabian asked as he pulled out his M1911 .45 caliber pistol with a suppressor attached to it, and pointed it at the lock attached to the roof door.

"Well, for one, the boss said to shoot him in the head and let his body rot. And two, and most importantly, the boss is going to be pissed, because fuck ups like these bring a lot of bad heat. I mean, it does make us look bad after all."

"How so? The cocksucker is dead isn't he?" Fabian replied.

"Yeah Fabe, you're right, he is dead, but you're leaving out important factors here. For one, the douchebag laying on top of the car is duct taped to the chair, which could raise a red flag to the police," Frankie sarcastically explained.

"Not to mention, it makes us look bad to other potential clients who will view this, and say that we're unreliable. This was, after all, supposed to be clean," Frankie finished explaining to him as he backed away to allow Fabian to shoot the lock open.

After two failed attempts at shooting the lock, Fabian, disturbed by his inability to shoot at something as simple as a lock, refused to look at his brother and best friend, who were clearly laughing to themselves.

"Perhaps you'd like for me to go back to the apartment and get you the mirror."

"Fuck you, Sebastian!" Fabian yelled at his brother, embarrassed, as he inspected the bullet holes in the door.

"The two of you really need to chill the fuck out before someone hears us," Frankie told them, laughing when he realized the door was able to open without having to shoot the lock.

"Look at the bright side Fabe, you showed that door whose boss, good for you."

Frankie gave Fabian a sarcastic pat on the back and walked out onto the rooftop. He moved toward the edge to take a quick peek at the carnage down below.

"Oh shit, that son-of-a-bitch is still tied down to the chair," Frankie loudly whispered.

"Alright, let's get out of here, and go to that pizzeria. We'll order a pie and walk directly to the car, and get the hell out of here. I'm sure Khan, and Red, are waiting for our phone call," Sebastian anxiously reminded them as he scanned the rooftops to the neighboring buildings.

"Sebastian, I hope this works because I can't risk going to prison for this bullshit," Frankie said, with apprehension in his voice.

"No one is going to prison. Besides, we can't risk leaving the car there and having five-o randomly run the plates once they begin investigating. We need to beat them to the punch," Sebastian replied as he measured the distances between buildings.

"Ahh Sabastian, I don't know if you really noticed, but these buildings are not exactly close to one another. And in case you haven't been told recently, or you're in total fucking denial, but we're not in the greatest of shape," Frankie explained to him, trying to be reasonable.

"Fuck, Sebastian, you're not even listening are you?" Fabian asked, noticing his brother zone out, as he had done so many times before.

Attempting to snap Sebastian out of it, Fabian slowly started making his way back to the rooftop door and said, "Sebastian, the sun is just about to set. Perhaps we can find another way?"

"Look, you fucking pussies," Sebastian snapped. "You want to go back downstairs, go ahead, but I'm jumping!"

"Is anyone up there?" An old woman's voice shouted out from the floor below the apartment building.

The three accomplices, nervously stared at each other, ran back about twenty feet, and in synchronized motion, ran toward the edge of the building, leaped over the rooftop and crash-landed on the abrasive neighboring rooftop.

"Fuck, Frankie, I think I hurt my ankle," Sebastian hissed in pain.

"Shh. I think she's on the rooftop," Frankie whispered as he pointed to the rooftop they just jumped from, pushing them flat on their backs.

"Is anyone there?" the older woman called out loudly as she peeked her head out and cautiously scanned her rooftop.

"Damn kids," she said to herself as she closed the door and locked it, never taking notice of the bullet holes.

"How the fuck did she know we were up on the roof?" Sebastian asked as he painfully got up.

"She probably lives in the apartment below and heard us," Fabian explained also rising to his feet. He softly walked to the end of the other side of the roof and leaped over to the next building that was only feet away.

"Are you able to get up and walk?" Frankie asked, amused by Sebastian wincing.

"What the fuck are you laughing at, Frankie? I really could've gotten hurt!"

"Man, the way you landed and screamed like a bitch; that shit was fucking classic."

"Go ahead, Frankie. Call me a bitch one more time, I dare you!" Sebastian warned as he limped to the other side of the roof.

"Shut the hell up," Fabian loudly whispered to them as he scanned the surrounding rooftops, "We're not in the clear yet. The last thing I need is to get caught because of some out-of-shape, inept hitman."

"Inept? Fuck you, Fabian. You can't run a block without holding on to something so that you can catch your breath," Sebastian angrily retorted.

"Look, that door is open on the other side," Fabian pointed out, "We need to make one final jump and we'll be in the clear."

Fabian and Frankie, both eyed look at Sebastian, who was clearly in pain, and gave him a look.

"Oh, don't worry about me, I'll make it," Sebastian reassured them. He walked several paces back, ran forward made a pathetic leap to the other side, and landed on his backside, snapping his suppressor off his gun.

"Damn," Fabian commented, looking at Frankie, who did everything in his power not laugh.

"Oh well, let's go."

Both Fabian, and Frankie, who were able to successfully leap and land on their feet, smiled at each other, and stared at Sebastian, who was still lying on his back, trying to toughen out the pain.

"Come on Sebastian, let's get you up," Frankie said to him, genuinely feeling bad.

"Hey man, I think we're good," Fabian whispered out as he motioned them from the rooftop doorway.

"Alright, like I said earlier, let's cautiously walk downstairs, walk out the backyard, enter the building behind us, and then exit out," Sebastian, explained to them in a pained voice as he tried to gather his composure.

"Are you alright, hop-along-Cassidy?" Frankie asked Sebastian, causing Fabian to chuckle.

"You know what? Fuck the both of you. I'm heading downstairs, crossing over to the other side of the building, exiting the hell out, heading to the pizzeria, and after that, I'm going to get my old man's car," he said to them annoyed. He then sat on the top of the staircase, removed his shoe and sock and revealed his ankle that was beginning to massively swell.

"Sounds like a plan, Sebastian," Frankie replied with a questionable look. "Let's get the hell out of here."

As the three covertly made their way down the stairs, they heard the sound of peep-hole cover's sliding back and forth. Realizing that their presence was known, they started feeling edgy and apprehensive.

"Shit," whispered Fabian.

"Don't worry about that and whatever you do don't look at the doors," Sebastian advised them.

"Sebastian, I hope that basement door is open because I am not feeling right about any of this shit," Frankie cautiously commented. He discretely unsnapped his hostler, preparing himself for any subtle opening of doors.

"Just keep your head tucked down and move quickly," Fabian whispered. As he realized that his older brother was struggling to walk down the stairs he stopped him from moving forward and asked, "Sebastian, we're almost there. Are you going to make it?"

"Yeah, let's just get this over with."

"Is that a fucking dog I hear?" Frankie nervously asked. He slowly walked toward the stairway window and peeked his head out. "Man, that is a really big dog. How the fuck are we going to get past that fucking beast?"

"I really don't give a shit. I'll shoot the fucking thing if I have to."

"Really, Fabian? You're are going to shoot a defenseless animal? An animal that is only trying to defend its territory?" Frankie asked Fabian.

"Take a look at Mr. fucking PETA over here," Fabian sarcastically replied. "I tell you what Frankie, why don't you telepathically speak to the fucking pooch and tell it to leave, so that we can cross over to the other side?"

"Oh yeah, when was the last time you shot at a dog? As a matter of fact, when was the last time you shot any animal?" Frankie scathingly asked Fabian.

"Do you have a better idea, Frankie?" Sebastian asked him, signs of agitation covering his face.

"Look, all I'm saying is that killing the dog isn't going to help things. People are weird when it comes to animals. They'd rather see people get shot and killed than to see a dog go through that."

"Well Frankie under our current circumstances we don't have the luxury of placing great consideration on if the dog is going to live or not," Fabian explained as he removed his .45 and screwed on a silencer.

"Okay, on the count of three, I'm going to open the door, let the dog in, shoot the fucking thing, and we'll swiftly walk to the other side," Fabian told both of them directing his attention at Frankie.

"Don't worry about him, he'll get over it. Just open the door and shoot the fucking thing, I'm in pain here," Sebastian said as he removed a long knife and braced himself.

"One, two..."

"Are you really going to hurt my dog?" A young girl questioned as she stood on top of the staircase with what was obviously a walking cane.

The three accomplices, who were initially startled, remained silent as they stared at the girl in total disarray.

"I know the three of you are still here, because you're all heavily wearing really bad smelling cologne, not to mention my dog is still barking."

"Can we help you, little girl?" Sebastian cautiously asked.

"As matter of fact you can. You can start by not shooting my dog and letting me take her back upstairs to my place."

Frankie, who flashed a big smile at Fabian, waved his hand from side to side to confirm if the girl was blind.

"What's your dog's name?" Frankie asked as he motioned to Fabian to put his gun away.

"Lacy. I always bring her out here so that she can go to the bathroom. She's a good dog. She won't harm you."

"Little girl, why don't you take the dog out through the front instead of the backyard?" Fabian softly asked.

"Because I'm blind you stupid son-of-a-bitch. In case you haven't figured it out," she sarcastically responded. "The backyard is small, there are no cars, and I can feel my way around a lot easier."

Sebastian and Frankie didn't know whether they should laugh or harshly respond, and stood looking at Fabian, who showed obvious signs of defeat for he knew he was rightfully burned.

"How are you going to remove your dog without a chain?" Sebastian asked.

"Well, it's pretty obvious you geniuses' don't pay attention to detail, but my dog chain is hanging on the door hinge. I leave it there so that I can easily find it."

Frankie, who immediately looked at Sebastian and smiled as he thought about Fabian's unnecessary door lock shooting incident just minutes ago.

"Go ahead, little girl. Go get your dog," Frankie said to her as the three cleared the way for her to walk.

"The three of you really need to change colognes. It's probably the reason why Lacy is barking so much," she told them, revulsion in her voice as she felt around the door hinge, grabbed the leash and walked outside.

The dog immediately ceased its territorial barking once it saw its owner, which eased any apprehension the three amigos had; that is, until an extremely large head of a one hundred and thirty pound Rottweiler peaked its head in from the cracked-open door.

"Shit Frankie, look at the head on that fucking dog," Fabian whispered as he slowly reached for his pistol and eased his body to the corner.

Frankie, who never thought twice about hurting or even killing a human being, felt differently about animals. He had a profound love for them, especially dogs, and was not going to allow Fabian to shoot the dog, especially after it showed no signs of aggression.

"No!" Frankie whispered out, hoping not to startle the dog and its blind owner.

"You see. Lacy is of no harm to any of you, so do us a favor and leave. Oh, and one more thing, take that dreadful smell with you," she scathingly told them as she walked her dog close to her hip.

Sebastian, who could not believe the incomprehensible event that just unfolded, looked at his brother and his childhood best friend and gazed at them in confusion. They soaked in the situation several seconds and watched the little girl without incident, walked up the stairs with her K-9 companion, and go back inside her apartment.

"Do we really smell that bad?" Fabian asked, distressed, as he smelled his shirt and armpits.

"She was referring to our cologne, not your body odor you dumb fuck," Sebastian said to his brother. He began to limp outside the doorway, leading them into the courtyard with a direct path to the building behind them.

"Oye, that little girl just standing there without making a sound was pretty creepy, don't you think? Like brujeria creepy," Fabian commented. The very vision of her standing on top of the staircase without saying a word just staring, freaked him out.

"Look, let's just get the hell out of here, walk to the pizzeria and get the car. This day is shot," Frankie said as he picked up his pace and reached the backdoor entrance that would lead them to the opposite side of the neighborhood street.

"Frankie, go in and make sure that it's clear to walk in, and please don't shoot anyone," Sebastian ordered.

"Why do I have to do it? Why can't you do it?"

"Well, for beginners, I'm not the most mobile right-about-now, and secondly and most importantly, my little brother is experiencing some aiming issues. So please with fucking cherries covered on top, can you make sure that it's clear to walk in and exit out?"

"Sebastian, I am not in the mood to listen to your bullshit right now. So help me God, I will fuck up your other ankle," Fabian snapped.

"The two of you need to shut the fuck up. And Fabian, please don't use the lord's name that way."

"Well isn't this great, a killer with a fucking conscience," Fabian replied frustrated.

"I am not going to argue with you because it's pointless, so hang tight. I'll be back you freaking fags," Frankie shot back before running into the apartment building.

"Damn, look at this place Sebastian, this is a bad place to get caught by the good and bad guys," Fabian pointed out as he viewed the alleyway that merged all the apartment building together.

"Yeah, you're right. The peeping eyes and silhouetted faces behind the curtains and in the darkened windows don't help either," Sebastian added, both brothers reserving themselves from displaying any type of uneasiness.

They initially calmly waited for the signal from there comrade to indicate that the coast was clear, but began losing patience with every passing minute, Just as they were about to enter the building prematurely.

"Psst…psst…Oye, pendejos, come on," Frankie whispered from a darkened backdoor entrance.

"Frankie, did you clear this area? You know that these gangways are infested with hostiles; hostiles that would love to see us disappear," Fabian reminded him as he peeked his head around to look for any potential threats.

"We're good. This will lead us into California, just a couple of blocks from Humboldt Park."

"Frankie, I know where we're at, we grew up in the motherfucker. What I am asking is, is it clear of both friend and foe?"

"Fabian, if you don't like how I cleared a path for us, do us all a favor and do it yourself next time."

"Shut the fuck up, you stupid fuck," Sebastian intervened. "Do you think he would do that to us?"

Fabian, about to lose his cool, looked at Frankie, who was obviously annoyed, and said, "Hey man I'm sorry. I'm just nervous, that's all."

"Fuck that and fuck you, Fabian. When we get out of this shit, you and I are going to have a little talk," Frankie said to him in a challenging manner.

"So how are we going to do this?" Fabian asked, dismissing Frankie's banter.

"I'm going to head in first and make sure that everything is still clear, then Sebastian will come in second and hop his ass in; and Fabian, you'll come in after covering our six. Once we accomplish this, we'll walk out to the pizza shop on Division and walk back to get your old man's ride."

"Fuck, Sebastian, I hope this crazy idea of yours works," Fabian said to his brother as he and Frankie racked their pistols and made sure their silencers were secured.

"What the fuck, Sebastian, you want everyone to hear you?" Fabian asked him noticing that his silencer was not on."

"The shit snapped off when I fell on the roof."

"You mean when you busted your ass and fell like a bitch," Frankie laughed as he began to make his way toward the gangway.

As the three began walking the narrow gangways corridors that lead them to their escape, each was individually reminded of their childhood when they all would have to cut through the various gangways to get to Roberto Clemente Community Academy.

The gangways environment, which was often consumed by poor sanitary conditions, and gallons of blood spilled throughout generations, sent a chill up their spines, as the odor from what they phrased as kids; the smell of death, funneled between the aging buildings, carried in the chilled air.

"How the fuck did we manage to grow up here and survive?" Fabian whispered to himself. But his brother, who was feeling the same sentiment, heard him as if it was spoken loudly.

"I don't know, Fabe. All I know is that I refuse to have children because of this shithole," Sebastian replied.

Division Street, was eerily clear of automotive and foot traffic, stopping them immediately at the foot of the exit point, Humboldt Park in view.

"I don't know about you guys, but all this walking, jumping, and sneaking around made me hungry," Sebastian commented to them and tucked his pistol away after sensing all was good. He began to slowly walk forward.

Never looking behind him, a self-taught habit that was formed throughout the years, Sebastian, sensing that he was free of any police involvement and inconspicuously limped his way to the local pizzeria as planned.

"You know your brother has some major fucking issues," Frankie said to Fabian who was looking at the surrounding building in search for any potential hostile.

"Yeah, he does, but you have to admit that he is one lucky son-of-a-bitch, or God just favors him."

"I don't think we need to be adding God to this conversation. With our questionable past, I'd be surprised if we would even be worthy of standing before him on our day of judgment."

"Jeez Frankie, was all that necessary?"

"I just don't want to be a hypocrite about it, Fabe," Frankie said to him as the two walked out from the bowels of Chicago's hell, and followed Sebastian, who was about twenty feet away.

Fabian, thought about Frankie's comment and questioned his own mortality; a sentiment that riddled his thoughts from time-to-time, making him feel uncomfortable. "So you think we are going to hell, Frankie?"

"Truthfully, I don't know where we're going, but if you were God, would you consider forgiving guys like us?"

"Damn, Frankie, why do you have to bring up shit like that for?"

"You're the one that brought up God and how he favors your brother. I just kept it real."

"I know, but..."

"Look, Fabian, despite all your nonsense and me wanting to kick your ass, and I really do want to kick your ass, you're like a brother. I love you man, but let's be honest, working our way up and being recognized as the people we are today, and having a conscience about it, just do not go hand in hand."

Fabian, who was obviously conflicted and had no other choice but to accept what was morally factual, remained silent as the proverbial world that surrounded him appeared for the first time, discouraging. It was a feeling that did not settle well with him until he reached the pizzeria.

"I'm going to get the usual for us, so while I'm waiting, go ahead and call Khan," Sebastian asked of his brother as he and Frankie entered the pizzeria. "Don't explain to him in great detail about what took place or how it ended, just tell him that all is good."

* *

"Todo está bien?" (All is good?)
"Si."
"Estás seguro?" (Are you sure?)
"Por supuesto." (Of course)
"Fabe, I need you to listen to me closely, do you understand?"

Fabian who immediately sense that something was seriously wrong, remained quiet as his stomach started to rumble, the way it has done since he was a little boy when something was wrong.

"What's up, Khan?"
"Whose apartment did you go to today?"
"Stelios, just like you asked me too. Why?"
"Are you sure that's who you met up with?"
"Yeah."
"Fabian, are you sure?"

"Khan, you gave me the name of the bar he hangs out at. We all scoped out the area for several hours, and followed him to an apartment like you asked."

"What did he look like Fabian?"

"Mild complexion, dark hair, thick eyebrows, you know, like a typical Greek guy. Why?"

"Are you sure he wasn't Guinea?"

"What the fuck are you talking about, Khan?"

"Fabian, are you sure you didn't confuse our target with a Guinea?"

"Kahn, if you placed Greeks, Guinea's and most Puerto Ricans together, we all look the fuck alike."

"Fabian, our person of interest was supposed to be Stelios Papadopoulos. Instead, the fucker on top of the car is Lorenzo Giordano."

Fabian, who was a little confused by his unexpected information, looked into his pocket to verify the address and became stressed when he realized that the address they were supposed to go to was about a mile away.

"So then…whose apartment did we go to?" Fabian asked inquisitively.

"I really don't know. This guy Stelios has been banging some Puerto Rican chick that worked at the bar where he hangs out at, it's possible it was her apartment," Khan explained.

"So how did we get the wrong guy?"

"Well, it turns out that this Lorenzo guy has been banging her as well," Khan added.

"Fuuuuuck!" Fabian replied in astonishment. "Oh well, I guess we're going to have to head back and go to the right address."

"It's pretty damn obvious that you don't recognize the name, so let me enlighten you. Lorenzo Giordano is an up and coming man who should have never been touched."

"Is he with a family?"

"Yeah Fabian, you can say something like that, or you can say that he is the nephew of Antonio Mancini, and happens to be one of the captains from the Giordano crime family. The same family that has been consistently hiring us for years now."

"How is that even possible Khan? Wasn't that Lorenzo kid like a fat fuck?"

"Perhaps the very concept of people losing weight is mind-boggling to you right now, however this Stelios Papadopoulos is Lorenzo's best friend and was the intended man of interest. It was specifically requested by Mr. Mancini because of Stelios out-of-control gambling debt.

"Oh shit Khan, what are we going to do?"

"I don't think they know it was us at this moment, but that shit will change shortly, especially when they find out that that it was someone from this family that placed the hit."

"Khan, you're confusing the hell out of me. I thought Mancini asked us to do it as a favor for him?"

"It is a favor…I mean…look, it's just too complicated, and right now the less you guys know the better off you will be. And speaking of the boss, he is pissed the fuck off. Fabe,

I don't know where you are, but you need to get your ass over here; like right now!"

"Khan, we drove dad's car near the apartment and it's parked there," Fabian told him, leaving out the part where Lorenzo Giordano almost landed on it.

"Fabe, I don't want to hear you right now or know about anything in addition to what I already know. You, Sebastian and Frankie better correct this issue and get your asses over here now!" khan screamed out in frustration.

Fabian, whose hands immediately began to tremble when he ended the call gravely looked at Frankie. It was a look that revealed that they had fucked up.

"What's up?" Frankie asked him as he lit up a cigarette.

"Frankie, we fucked up. We got the wrong guy."

"What do you mean, we got the wrong guy?"

"The guy who jumped out was Lorenzo Giordano."

"Lorenzo...Lorenzo, damn that name sounds familiar. Wait a minute, isn't that Lorenzo guy like a fat fuck?" Frankie asked with a questioning look.

"Yeah...yeah he was," Fabian replied as he stared with a blank look.

"Well shit Fabian," he said with a little chuckle, "That's more than a wrong guy."

"Frankie, that was Antonio Mancini's nephew."

"Oh shit," Frankie said, still laughing. "This is not good. We better get your brother. He's going to shit himself when he finds all this shit out."

"Frankie, what are we going to do?"

"Well, before we say anything let's eat first. I am starving."

Fabian, who could not believe that Frankie was not even showing any signs of distress, bowed his head in defeat, and inhaled deeply. "We are probably going to have to go into hiding because of this shit."

"Does anyone know it was us?" Frankie asked.

"Khan isn't sure. He doesn't think so, but the boss knows."

"How?"

"It's too complicated, but we need to head over there as soon as possible and get the car away from that crime scene."

"Well, like I said, please wait until I at least get a slice in before telling your brother."

"Frankie, you have some serious fucking issues, man."

"No, Fabian, we all do, and stressing over all this shit on an empty stomach is going to make it even worst."

"Let's go," Fabian said, mentally preparing how to explain to his brother that they got the wrong guy; (an act that was sure to come with consequences, especially when Sebastian repeatedly asked to confirm his identity).

Fabian, who became extremely troubled as he neared his brother patiently waiting for him and Frankie with a fresh pizza pie, was unable to make eye contact with his brother; a recognizable reaction, Sebastian knew all too well, that something was not right.

"Alright, Sebastian," Frankie happily said, rubbing his hands together as the aroma escaping the pizza box aroused his appetite.

"What the fuck, can't you wait till we get in the car to eat?" Sebastian asked as he placed the pizza box on the hood of a car.

"Sebastian, we were waiting in the car for that homocrat, unibrow-sporting, Olive-picking nigger for hours. Not to mention we've been jumping rooftops, and dealing with blind little girls. So forgive me if I built up an appetite," Frankie said, pulling apart a slice.

"What about you, Fabe, you want a slice?" Sebastian asked as he noticed his brother sweating.

"Is everything alright? Is there something I need to know, or something that was said between you and Khan?"

"Look I was going to tell you as soon as Frankie finished eating."

"Shit, you can tell him all that was said, I'm good Fabian," Frankie said with a mouth full of pizza.

"What the fuck are you going to tell me, Fabian?"

With a disappointed look that immediately worried his brother, Fabian took a deep breath and fixed his eyes on the ground. "We got the wrong guy."

"What the fuck do you mean we got the wrong guy?"

"Well, the guy we were supposed to whack is Stelios Papadopoulos. Apparently, he owed a lot of money."

"So what does that mean that we need to find this Stelios prick and polish him off?" Sebastian asked, clearly annoyed.

"I don't know yet, we were told to come in to see the boss," Fabian softly replied.

"Tell him the other pile of shit we just stepped into," Frankie intervened as he shoved another slice into his mouth.

"What other shit? What is he talking about?" Sebastian asked with a concerned look in his eye.

"You know the idiot that jumped out the window?"

"No. I don't know who the fucking idiot was Fabe. Was that supposed to be a rhetorical question?"

"No."

"So just tell me, who was the fucking jerk-off that landed face first on the hood of a car?"

"Lorenzo Giordano"

"Fuck, that name sounds familiar. Is this someone we need to be worried about?" Sebastian asked as he placed his face in his hands.

"He's Antonio Mancini's Nephew."

"Antonio Mancini? The same Antonio Mancini who is the captain of the Ricci crime family?"

Fabian, couldn't look his brother directly in the eye, and instead bowed his head with apprehension.

"Fuck this, I am not taking the fucking rap for this shit. You're the one who killed him, not me."

"Well technically, we never killed him. The dumb fucker jumped out of the window on his own will." Frankie explained.

"Well, technically you're a fucking idiot," Sebastian mockingly said to his younger brother.

"So now we have to go get dad's car, go over to the boss's house and potentially prepare for war? Is that what you're telling me?"

"Sebastian, we really didn't kill him."

"Fabian, shut the fuck up. You're starting to sound as callous as this fucking half-Cuban, half-polack crazy motherfucker over here.

"Whoa...whoa...whoa...I resent that polack comment. You don't hear me talk about Puerto Ricans that way."

"Shut the fuck up," both Fabian and Sebastian yelled at him.

"Fabe, this is some fucked up shit you got us into. I should just walk away and leave you to deal with this shit."

"I know, Sebastian, but I can't do this without you. And you too, Frankie. I can't do this without you both."

"You don't have to worry about me," Frankie assured him. "I don't give a fuck about these fucking pricks. I mean, what the fuck they have ever done for me, or any of us, other than placing us in fucked up situations since we were kids."

Fabian, who appreciated his friend's loyalty, turned to his brother and watched him nervously pace back and forth. "Sebastian, I'm sorry, but you know if it were you, I would be there for you."

"Does Red know?" Sebastian asked.

"Sebastian, I really don't know who does at this point. All I know is that the wrong guy is dead, dad's car is at the crime scene, and Khan just told me the boss wants us to get our asses over there. And if we don't go, our brother could potentially get whacked himself."

"Well that's it, we all have to see the boss," said Sebastian.

"Whoa...whoa...whoa, first of all, that Jew fuck is not my boss. He might be your boss, but not mine. And secondly, you mentioned they didn't know that it was us, right?" Frankie asked with a defensive tone.

"Well Khan wasn't sure; at least that's what he made it sound like."

"Fabian, either he said they did know or they didn't know; which one was it?"

"He said he doesn't think they know it was us," Fabian said.

Sebastian, stared at his brother with disappointment as his mind raced. He kept thinking to himself that if it were him in that predicament, his little brother would have had his back; a sentiment he also felt towards his brother Khan and his best friend's Frankie and Red.

"Frankie, give me the pizza box. Let's start walking toward the car and act surprised when we arrive because by now, that shit is taped off."

"No, Sebastian, I'll do it. I got us into this mess and I will get us out of it."

"How, Fabian, by mumbling your way out of it?" Sebastian asked him.

Frankie started to laugh and said in agreement with Sebastian's comment, "When you get nervous, you start to mumble like a fucking tard, so do yourself a favor and let your bother handle this. We'll just follow his lead.

Fabian, who was extremely grateful, silently agreed. His eyes began to water because he knew that this was just the beginning. They were potentially facing some real trouble that could turn into an ugly and unnecessary war.

* *

"Oh, what the fuck. I park here for twenty minutes and this shit happens," Sebastian yelled out as he neared the car with a pizza box in his hands, watching Chicago's finest taking photos of an apparent suicide.

"This your car?" the police officer rudely asked him.

"No, but the one next to it is. What the fuck happened?"

"An angel bound to a chair fell from heaven and landed on a car. What the fuck does it look like just happened?" the officer sarcastically replied.

"Well can I take my car out of there? I have to be somewhere."

"What, are you fucking kidding me? Can't you see that this is a crime scene?"

"Is that blood on my bumper?" Sebastian added pissing off the officer further.

"Look, you stupid son of a bitch, if you disrupt our investigation in any way, I will arrest you for tampering with evidence, obstruction, and for being an asshole."

"Officer, I just want to get the hell out of here. This shit is not cool you know?"

"Just back away and let us handle our business."

"Oh shit, what the fuck happened?" Frankie joined in as he and Fabian arrived shortly after making it seem like they had been waiting on Sebastian for a long time.

"I don't know. This poor guy jumped I guess and landed near the car with my rag top down, mind you, and now they won't let me drive off," Sebastian complained.

"Officer, we need to be across town at an important event and we really need that car. Can we please take our car and get out of your way so that you can conduct your investigation?" Frankie asked the officer, attempting to reason with him.

"I don't give a shit where you guys need to be. The car isn't going anywhere until I'm told it's okay to do so."

"Hey, aren't you Malone?" Fabian asked, looking at the officer as if he remembered him from somewhere.

"Who wants to fucking know?" the officer gruffly responded.

"Don'tcha remember me?"

"Should I?"

"Well, maybe not. Back then I was, and still am, a nobody. But you and I used to be in the same class at Roberto Clemente."

Malone, took a long look at Fabian and ran his face through a mental database, but did not remember him. He did, however, settle down as Fabian brought up events that could have taken place; especially since he attended Roberto Clemente.

"Yeah, I remember you," Fabian added. "There was one time you and I spent time in detention in Mrs. Fletcher's class."

The officer always had trouble remembering names and faces. He did spend time in detention, but did not remember Fabian.

"What's your name?" Malone asked, making one final attempt at remembering anything Fabian claimed to have happened.

"Eric Alvarez," Fabian responded, using a name of a deceased kid he once knew in high school. "Look, we know that this is a messed up situation, and this is out of your control. We will just leave, come back another day for the car and get to where we have to another way."

"Let me talk to my Lieutenant. If they're okay with you taking the car, you can go."

"Officer Malone, thank you," Fabian replied, his voice full of respect.

The brothers and Frankie spent several minutes patiently waiting and watching a steady stream of spectators hovering around and taking photos of the corpse's body. Fabian, who pretended not to be disturbed by the events that were taking place, nonchalantly inspected every detail on what he had believed was his intended target body.

"Frankie, doesn't this fucking Guinea look like that goat humper? I mean fuck, look at him."

"I don't give a shit if it's him or not, Fabian. All I know is that we need to get the fuck out of here before someone figures us out."

"Oh shit I think he is missing his eyeballs," Sebastian pointed out. Instinctively they were all forced to quickly look around the street and see if the eyeball might have popped out.

"Maybe they're under the car," Frankie commented.

"Oh shit, that would be some fucked up shit," Fabian whispered with a slight chuckle.

"I wouldn't be laughing too much if I were you Fabe. We are all here going through this bullshit because of you," Sebastian said to him as they watched an ambulance pull up.

"Does anyone know who this car belongs to?" a paramedic yelled out to some nearby officers.

"Yeah, it belongs to me," Sebastian answered.

"Well, sir, we're going to have to ask you to please move it out. We're about to remove the body and we cannot have it in here in our way," the paramedic explained placing a smile on the three accomplices.

"Well, the officer said we cannot move it," Sebastian responded.

"Go ahead, you're good," Officer Malone said to them as he walked back over.

"Thank you, officer."

"No, thank him," the officer said pointing at the paramedic. "Because if it were up to me, it would have stayed here. Now get the fuck out of here."

Sebastian, displayed a child-like smirk that showed egotism, as he opened the door and inattentively threw a pizza box into the seat stared at Officer Malone, who was clearly aggravated.

Frankie, who showed little concern, especially about the deceased, gaily patted Sebastian on the shoulder as he climbed into the car.

"Motherfuckers," the officer muttered to himself.

"Officer Malone, I thank you for what you do. Be safe out there," Fabian said to him, breaking the officer's unpleasant attentiveness toward his brother and Frankie.

The officer, who was clearly upset, imperceptibly stared at the two brothers and best friend as they calmly drove away from the crime scene.

Chapter II

A Deadly Ass Chewing

"Please, whatever you do, do not say anything stupid, insulting, derogatory or disrespectful to Avvi. Today is not that day. This shit is serious!" Khan sternly explained to his two adoptive brothers and best friend.

"Do you really think we would do that?" Fabian asked as he was led by Khan down the corridor leading to Avner Levine's office at his private gentlemen's club.

"Sebastian, explain to this stupid motherfucker that his opinion or comment is not worth anything right now. As a matter of fact, remind this clueless fuck that it is because of him that we're in this situation. So please, tell him to shut the fuck up, because he obviously doesn't comprehend the gravity of this situation."

"But."

"Fabian, shut the fuck up," Sebastian shouted, cutting him off before entering Avner's office.

"Yo, Fabe, Khan is right. Just let the Jew fuck yell a little and after he's done, let's get the fuck out of here. I'm starting to get a fucking headache," Frankie said, annoyed as he was about to walk in the office.

"You just don't get it do you, Frankie," Khan said blocking him from entering. "This is fucking serious. What happened today can potentially lead to a nasty, drawn-out war, and the last I remember, you're a one-man army nobody gives a shit about,"

"We got it, Khan," Sebastian said, placing his hand on his shoulder, defusing the hostile intensity. "None of us wants war."

Khan, who starting to show signs of being stressed out, sighed as he bowed his head, and allowed the three to enter the office.

"Khan, can I make a drink?" Fabian asked.

"Sit the fuck down, stupid son-of-a-bitch," Sebastian said in anger.

"Can someone explain to me what the fuck happen today?" Avner shouted, as he entered his office, escorted by his longtime associate Abner Horowitz, and personal henchman, Sean "Red" McLoughlin.

"And, by the way, since you are obviously having a fucking hard time figuring shit out, do me a favor and shut the fuck up because I do not want to hear any bullshit from you, you sorry fuck!" Avner shouted at Fabian, red-faced.

"We got the wrong man, Mr. Levine," Frankie calmly explained.

"You know I've been in this business for forty-two undisruptive years," Avner said as he lit up a cigarette. "And never not once; and let me remind you that I have dealt with some shlimazel's in my time, have I ever ran into such trouble. But you schlumps took it to another level."

"But, Avvi…"

"Didn't I just explain to your brother that I don't want to hear his shit just a few moments ago?" Avner asked Khan, who had his head down.

"Yes, you did."

"Then why is he talking to me? Can anyone explain that to me?" Avner angrily shouted.

"Now, as I was explaining before I was rudely interrupted," he continued, "Never not once, have I ever seen or have I ever been placed in this situation. Now I have to make some serious decisions here, decisions that can potentially fix or break relationships."

An unnerving silence filled the room. The Rodriguez brothers, Frankie and Red, all instinctively gazed away from each other as the very possibility of someone being whacked, primarily Fabian, was a reality that none of them wanted to accept.

Red, had been a childhood friend and considered part of the Rodriguez extended family all of his life. He knew that if the order was made to take out Fabian, it was going to have to happen over Sebastian's body. And Frankie, who he knew did not give a shit about Avner, would also defend the only friends that would take a bullet for him.

"So what the hell happened out there? Why is the nephew of Mr. Mancini lying face down on top of some car, tied to a chair, outside the apartment of some Puerto Rican broad he's been banging?"

As Avner looked around at the still faces surrounding his solid oak executive desk, he grew disenchanted by their carelessness, because they should have known better. He leaned back in his chair, took a deep drag of his cigarette, then, leaned forward again and smacked the table with the palm of his hand.

"Somebody better fucking say something because this is not going to get swept under the rug and be forgotten about," he yelled before his anger turned to nervousness. "Do you guys realize I'm left out here vulnerable? Somehow, someway, they're going to come to me for answers."

Then, like a sudden storm, a hail of bullets unleashed deliberate dominance and obliteration in the room. The gunfire breached the wood, glass, and anything in its path, interrupting the safety that once was Avner's office.

The abrasive intrusion forced all of the room's occupants to drop to the ground for cover. Avner screamed out in horror as shards of glass rained over his body and his haven of life' simple's pleasures, turned into a reality of doom.

"Avvi, are you okay?" Red yelled out as he assessed the smoky surroundings that smelled of gunpowder.

"Is anyone hit?" Red yelled out again as the feathers from Avner's exotic birds he kept in his office caught his attention. He started breathing rapidly at the frightening scene of the animals remains, innocently shredded during the melee, and now landing on the body of Avner's longtime associate, Abner.

"Avvi, we gotta get you out of here," Red said, covering his body in case a second round of gunfire made its way through again.

"What happened?" Avner asked, with a raspy voice, gasping for air.

Red quickly inspected Avner's body and saw that he was hit near his shoulder and abdomen. Immediately he knew this was a retaliation from the Ricci crime family; a sobering reminder to Red about the complexities of the business he chose to follow.

"Avvi, Avvi..." several people called out from the floor below, as they raced up the stairs coming to Avner's aid.

"What the hell happened? Is the old man alright?" one of Avner's lieutenants, Heiman Blasberg, yelled out as he rushed in.

Sebastian and Frankie looked between the window that was completely shot off then looked at each other in amazement. They knew that it should have been them cut down and laying in their own pool of blood, on the floor of the disarrayed office.

"Frankie, how is this even possible?" Sebastian asked him, shocked.

"I don't know, but this shit is not good."

"Fabian are you okay?" Sebastian fearfully called out.

"Fabe?" Frankie added.

"He's okay, Sebastian," Red yelled out. "But I think he is a little freaked out. Give him a minute, you know how he is."

"Khan?" Sebastian asked after his other brother.

"Shut the fuck up, Sebastian!" Khan whispered loudly. "We don't know whose still out there."

As sirens started announcing the police's arrival, Khan looked at Avner lying lifeless on the floor and began to panic. He knew that from the get-go, all Avner wanted to do was get the full story so that he could find a way to fix the problem or redirect the blame.

"Avvi...Avvi...are you okay?" Heiman asked as he pulled Avner near the desk and away from the window. But Avner was slowly fading out. He tried to whisper something into his lieutenant's ear, but passed out as his body went into shock.

The room was filled with an eerie silence and the smell of death. Fabian was the first to stand and was asked by Heiman to scout the rooftop to see if he could find any hostiles.

Fabian raced up the stairs and visually cleared the rooftop. He gingerly walked toward the rooftop's edge, poked his head out for a better view and was relieved that nobody responsible for the attack had stuck around.

Sensing someone was standing at the rooftop doorway, Fabian turned to see who it was. He was not surprised when he saw Heiman staring aggressively at him.

"I'm no coward Heime. I, unlike my enemies, like to stare my victims in the face before I pull the trigger," Fabian said to him with intensity. He had the feeling that Heiman considered him responsible for the assault.

"How did anyone know that he was going to be in the office at that very moment?" Heiman asked Fabian, pointing a pistol at him.

"What the hell are you talking about, Heime?"

"How did anyone outside know that he was going to be in his office precisely at that moment?"

"You're kidding, right? You know what, Heime, maybe you had something to do with it?"

"What does that mean?" Heiman asked, cocking his .357.

"What it means is that my little brother had nothing to do with the spraying," Sebastian said, appearing behind Heiman and catching him off guard as he placed a gun to his head.

"Avvi has been there for over twenty years in the same room, and never, not once, has this ever happened," Heiman continued.

"You're right Heiman, but I can assure you that we had nothing to do with it," Sebastian explained. He focused his front sight directly at Heiman's head.

"So what are you going to do? Are you going to shoot me the way Avvi was shot?"

"Turn around, you stupid Jew fuck," Sebastian angrily ordered him. "I want to look at you in the eyes. I believe Fabian explained just moments ago that's how we do it."

Heiman reluctantly turned around and thought of several ways he could shoot his way out of there. He reminded himself that he had known the Rodriguez brothers for quite some time, and knew that they were not afraid to pull the trigger; especially Sebastian.

"We all have known that old man since we were kids. That man fought alongside our father in Vietnam. He was even there when our parents adopted Khan. That's not something a person overlooks," Sebastian said to Heiman with conviction.

The silence echoed with uncertainty as the three men stood on the rooftop, each of them filled with raw betrayal and hesitancy.

"What the fuck are you doing, Sebastian?" Khan screamed in shock. He and Frankie had reached the rooftop.

"Mr. Heiman here had his .357 pointed at Fabian's head."

"Sebastian, this isn't good."

"No fucking shit, Khan. I kind of picked up on that."

"Heime, you know us—we would never do this to the old man," Khan pleaded.

"Ahh, I don't know about all of that. That Jew-prick-fuck never liked me."

"Frankie, shut the fuck up," Khan yelled, never losing eye contact with Heiman.

"Heime, listen to me: you know us, we would never do such a thing," Khan continued pleading with him.

"I don't know what to believe right now. All I know is that if the boss dies, you all die!" Heiman immediately replied.

"What do you mean, 'if'? He's not dead?" Frankie questioned.

"He's still breathing for now," Khan replied to Frankie, keeping eye contact with Heiman.

"What about PD?" Sebastian asked.

"You know most of them are on the books," Khan explained. "But they can only stay downstairs for so long."

"So what the fuck does that mean?" Fabian asked. He started looking around to the surrounding buildings.

"What it means is that we're going to get the fuck out of here," said Sebastian.

"I fucking knew it. You little spic bitches are going to try to escape unnoticed. Well fuck all of you," Heiman yelled out as he slowly lifted his .357, forcing all of them to point their pistols his way.

"Please, Heime. I promise you that this will all get cleared up, but right now we all have to leave."

"Khan, if you are—and that's a big if—able to make it out of here, you and your bitch asses better never show your faces around here. I can assure you that the next time we meet, I will not be the one having all the lullabies pointed at me."

"Heime, for what it's worth, you will eat your words," replied Khan.

"No, I won't... But what I am going to do is make your soon-to-be-spic-ass-dead-fucks my bitches when this is over."

Khan saw the sincerity and the fire in Heiman's eyes. He could only smirk as the very idea of not being able to walk freely in his Chicago neighborhood became a reality.

"Well unless you're going to use that thing the way a real man would, stick it up your ass and get the fuck out of here before I change my mind, and we all go out blasting," Heiman said to Sebastian.

"You're not going to do that, you have too much to lose," Frankie arrogantly told Heiman, scanning surrounding rooftops for an out. "Besides, you know we're innocent, but it's cool."

"The only thing I know is that I'll be seeing your half-spic, half-polack ass—which, by the way, is a fucked up subhuman mix—in the very near future under different circumstances. The kind of circumstances that places a gratifying smile on my face."

"Fuck you, Heime! That's not a nice thing to say to a man that doesn't give a fuck about what you think," Frankie mocked, scanning the rooftops for a second time. He gave a final, "Adios, pendejo," before leaping off their rooftop and onto the next.

"Fuck, Fabian, I'm getting tired of this jumping over the rooftops bullshit," Sebastian said to his brother. He forced his leg to swing over the edge of the rooftop, working to avoid re-aggravating his ankle, and jumped to the next building.

"I'll take this," Fabian said to Heiman as he took the lieutenant's pistol away. "And don't worry, I know how much you love this and will take good care of her.

"Khan, let's go," Fabian yelled. He kept his pistol aimed at Heiman, who, at this point, showed no sign of aggression.

Khan did not want to leave, but had no other choice but to stand by his brothers. He knew that if he chose to stay, the Ricci family would sanction his elimination, despite not having any proof of any of them being involved with Avner's attempted killing.

Like a thief in the night, Khan disappeared off the rooftop and into the late sunset that shadowed the narrow tree line. Heiman was unable to chase after them because he had to deal with the situation just floors below. He lit up a cigarette, walked to the edge of the building that faced the back side, and inspected the assault point.

"You want us to get 'em, boss?" one of Heiman's henchmen asked. He had entered the rooftop just in time to witness them escaping.

"No. Like cornered animals, they'll bite to protect themselves, and today they are cornered. Don't worry, we'll catch up with them in the future."

Chapter III

Dodging Heiman

After escaping without pursuit, the four comrades made it out into the dark, serene streets. They cautiously walked to their father's car, which was strategically parked several blocks away to avoid any potential strife. This tactic was taught by the brother's father who was always anxious when out in public, a result instilled from the Vietnam War.

"Why aren't they after us?" Fabian asked as they nervously walked the familiar neighborhood streets.

"Because that's the way Heime works," Khan snapped. "He lets you think you have the upper hand; then, when your guard is down, he strikes. You forget that he's been doing this for a long time."

"Well, we've taken folks out as well," Fabian tenaciously responded.

"Fabian, I love you man, you know I do, but you accidentally killing people as of late does not make you a hitman for hire."

"Screw you, Khan. They had it coming, and I made my employers happy," Fabian swiftly responded. His head snapped in the direction of Frankie and Sebastian who were chuckling at this claim.

"What the fuck you two jerk-offs laughing at?"

"I wouldn't hire you to serve drinks for a wedding, let alone hire you to whack someone," Frankie laughed.

"Oh yeah," Fabian angrily replied. He aggressively stepped up to Frankie, who was already waiting for him.

"What the fuck are you gonna do, you pretty motherfucker?" Frankie asked him, the hostility evident in his tone.

"The two of you need to chill the fuck out," Sebastian yelled as he forcefully separated them.

"Let me ask you a question, Fabian," Frankie heatedly said. "Do you think this Jew-fuck cocksucker gives a fuck about your inexperienced spic ass, or any of us?"

"Guys, let's keep a level head her," Khan intervened, nervously looking around at their surroundings.

"Shut the fuck up, Khan, and let Fabe get this bullshit out of his system," Sebastian responded, siding with Frankie.

"I know you've got the balls, and you'll do what you must, but this life isn't for you," Frankie said to Fabian.

"This Giordano family, or whatever they call themselves, wants to see us dead," Sebastian continued. "They will do everything in their power to accomplish that, including forcing Avvi's crew to make it happen, so do me a favor and don't lose sight of that."

As his older brother talked, Fabian started showing signs of being worried.

"A man like Heiman has no other choice but to hunt us down until we are brought forward to answer for this Lorenzo fuckup, dead or alive," Khan added, hoping to reason with Fabian. "Somehow, some way, we need to fix this bullshit. I don't know how, but it needs to happen. I don't want to die because of this nonsense."

"Let's go," Fabian said to them, finally coming to his senses. He realized that their situation just got real, and the only people he could count on were his brothers and Frankie.

"What about Red?" Sebastian asked. "Do you think he'll be ordered to make the hit on us?"

"Truthfully, I just don't know," Khan responded, full of apprehension.

"He's been with us since day one," Frankie added.

"Look, right about now he is scared shitless because of this very situation he might be forced into. And, if you think about it, he might have no other choice but to follow through," Sebastian said to them.

"So, what do we do now?" Frankie asked as he started to look up numbers on his phone.

"No, Frankie. Turn that shit off. As a matter of fact, get rid of the phone. That phone belongs to Avvi's operation and I'm sure he has that tracking device shit on it," Khan advised.

"They can do that?" asked Frankie, disappointed.

"I don't know if anyone from Avvi's crew is listening or tracking us this very second, but you know that Avvi has got a lot of blues and gowns under his payroll," Khan reminded him. "And I am more than certain that tracing us, or having the resources to make it happen, will not be an issue."

"But I like this phone. It has some of the coolest games…"

Like a scorned child about to have their favorite toy stripped away for bad behavior, Frankie stared sadly at the phone. Sebastian, aggravated by Frankie's inability to reason, took the phone way and aggressively tossed it to the side. He turned toward Frankie in a challenging manner and smiled as the phone landed, smashed to pieces.

"I am done fucking around with all of you," Sebastian said to them. "The two of you, give me your phone," he demanded of his brothers as he dug into his pockets in search of his own.

"As long as we don't have these things, we can't be located, right?"

"So now what?" Khan asked.

"Fabian, let's go to the club on California."

"Sebastian, you know me. Going to a club, especially at a moment like this, is not a very good idea. All that ass will only distract me."

"Yeah, fat asses," Frankie jabbed.

"Going to the club is pretty risky," Khan said to Sebastian.

"It is, that's why we're going to the rooftop, and we'll enter the club that way."

"What the hell is it today with the fucking rooftops? I mean, no offense to you Sebastian, but you really busted your ass today. As funny as that shit was, do you really think this is a good idea?" Fabian pointed out.

"Well, I guess you're saying it in a nice way because he's your brother, but what really happened is that he fell like a bitch today," Frankie rudely remarked.

"Damn, Sebastian, was it really like that today? I remember when you used to—"

"Go ahead, say one more thing about me, I fucking dare anyone right now to say anything stupid to me," Sebastian cut Khan off, heatedly threatening the group.

"Now shut the hell up and listen to the plan," he yelled out to them, continuing with an incensed glare. "We'll park several blocks away, walk toward the back parking lot near the club, gain access into a nearby building and cross over several rooftops until we reach the club."

"Damn, Sebastian, when did you start planning out these stupid covert operations of yours?"

"Fabian, are you serious? Do you not know your own neighborhood?"

"Well yeah, I know—"

"Shut the fuck up, Fabian. I really don't give a shit what you do or don't know," Sebastian snapped. He threw Fabian the keys as they approached the car.

Frankie and Khan chuckled at Sebastian's sarcastic banter, which demonstrated obvious signs of him losing his cool. The four entered the vehicle, racked their pistols and cruised down the street that was unusually quiet.

"Ahh shit," Sebastian whispered, realizing that he could not screw on a spare suppresser.

"What happened?" Khan asked, observing their surroundings nervously.

"Your brother busted his ass earlier today on a rooftop," Frankie explained.

"You had your silencer on when you were jumping from rooftop to rooftop?" Khan asked Sebastian, shocked. Sebastian refused to look at him.

"When we realized that we had no other choice but to make our escape from the rooftops, I decided to place my gun on my back, in case I had to shoot somebody," Sebastian tried to explain.

"And that's when he discovered jumping from rooftop to rooftop wasn't easy, especially with a pistol on your back," Fabian remarked, making the whole car roar with laughter.

"Just shut the hell up and take us to the club," Sebastian laughingly replied.

"Sebastian, on a serious level, do you think going to the club is a good idea?" Frankie asked. He knew Avvi had his imprint on several businesses in the general area.

"We're going to need some supplies, like cash, guns, and phones. We also need a place to stay, and keep in mind that it has to be outside of Chicago…as a matter of fact, outside the state of Illinois."

"You know, now that I think about it, I think we can go to my cousin's place in Pig's Eye Landing," Frankie explained to them as he removed his wallet and started searching for his cousin's number written on a business card.

"What the hell is Pig's Eye landing?" Fabian asked, looking at Frankie from the rearview mirror.

"Remember when my mom use to send me away for the summer as a kid so that she could keep me away from you douchebags? Well, she used to send me away to St. Paul's, Minnesota and many of the folks up there called it Pig's Eye Landing."

"That is the stupidest, gayest shit I have ever heard of," Fabian said to him, smiling with his brother Sebastian.

"Maybe so, but there are several bridges there off the Mississippi which will make it easy for us to leave in a hurry if we have to. Minneapolis isn't far from there and, most importantly, no one knows about the location. I mean, nobody."

"Are you sure?" Khan asked him.

"Did you guys know about it, or even have a clue that I used to go there? All you douchebags are my people, and none of you knew, so I think we'll be good there. Even if it is just temporary," replied Frankie with a smile, pulling out the card with his cousin's information written on it.

"You know, that might not be a bad idea, especially considering that Avvi hates the Vikings," Khan said with a pensive look.

"You know, now that I think about it, he really does hate that team. Why is that?" Sebastian asked.

"That's because he hates Canada and any state that touches Canada," Khan explained. "He would never go there or root for their team."

"I don't know. Aren't the winters pretty brutal up there?" Fabian debated.

"Any more stupid shit comes out of that fucking mouth of yours, and I'm going to club you like a fucking seal. Do you understand me?" Sebastian said angrily.

"What the fuck did I do now?" Fabian asked as he realized that his brother was serious.

"Are you fucking serious? What, it's not cold here in Chicago?" Sebastian questioned him.

"Goodness, Fabian," Khan said, shaking his head in disbelief.

"Park right here, and don't you say another word. You're starting to worry me," Sebastian said as he got out of the car. "Khan, Frankie, come with me; and Frankie, don't fuck this up by shooting someone," Sebastian warned.

"When have I ever shot anyone unjustifiably?"

Sebastian shared a knowing glance with Khan, then turned to stare at Frankie with an arguing look. He decided to dismiss Frankie's comment and continued with his last-minute planning.

"Fabian, go to our stash house and get our funds. There should be over a hundred K there, can you handle that?" Sebastian asked him as he looked around their surroundings to make sure there wasn't anyone suspicious.

Fabian slowly turned to look at his brother and smiled at him. Not long ago, he suggested they rent out an apartment so that they could save the money they obtained from a heist not long ago. "I can."

"Fabe, you need to keep your eyes open. It's open season on us, and any slip-ups will only hurt things. Do you understand?"

"I'll get it done"

"Once you get everything, come meet us here in this very spot so that we can leave right away," Sebastian explained as he lit up a cigarette.

"I'll need about thirty minutes."

"Good. That will give the three of us time to get all that we need."

After driving away and watching his brothers and Frankie from the rearview mirror, Fabian started realizing that it was going to be some time until he returned to the only home he had ever known. This knowledge developed in him a hankering to unload on his side-piece, Nora, a two hundred and eighty-pound woman he lovingly called Norca to the fellas.

"Man, I'm really pushing it if I asked her to meet me at the apartment," he said to himself as he waited for the light to change.

"Fuck it, she's only a couple of buildings away."

Having convinced himself, he pulled over to a payphone and made a quick call before heading to the safe house

Several minutes later, Fabian arrived at the safe house. He had an eerie feeling that someone was watching him, and drove around his surroundings to make sure it was clear.

"Why were you circling the neighborhood like that, are you in trouble?" Nora asked as she patiently waited for him at the entrance.

Fabian, who really admired her subtle beauty, kissed her and became immediately aroused by her lightly scented skin. "I'm going to fuck the shit out of this woman," he thought to himself, admiring his voluptuous delight walking up the stairs.

"Fabe, I only have a few minutes. I'm meeting up with my girlfriend and some friends. We're heading to that riverboat casino in Elgin," she explained as they entered the apartment.

"Sweetheart, I promise you it won't take long," he replied.

The two stumbled into the only bedroom inside the apartment. Fabian was mentally lost for a few seconds, staring passionately into her eyes.

"What's wrong, Fabian?" she asked, staring at his massive erection while removing her dress.

"Don't you ever feel bad about how your dyke girlfriend would feel if she ever found out? I mean, she hates me because, deep down, she knows that Fabester has been up that ass several times."

"Several times? Really, Fabian? You've been up my ass for several years now. Besides, she works night shift and is busy licking other women; I'm sure of it."

"Well, since you put it that way, may the fucking begin," he replied.

Fabian was naturally strong and able to lift her up and toss her in the twin-sized bed that showed signs of fatiguing beyond its limits. The pair commenced with blissful sexual indulgence, lasting for over twenty minutes.

"Nora, I have to leave and probably won't be back for some time," he said to her as he nervously began to dress.

"Where are you going?"

"As of right now, I'm not really sure. But I promise I'll stay in touch when I have the chance," he promised as he grabbed the bag of cash, He removed five thousand dollars and handed it to her.

"I'm not a whore, Fabian."

"Nora, I have and never will consider you a whore. But I care about you sincerely; always have."

"Fabian, you're scaring me."

"Believe me when I tell you that you that I'll be okay. But for now, I have to leave town," he amorously said, placing the cash in her hands.

"I can't take this, Fabian."

"Yes, you will, Nora. And I promise, when this is all over, I'll come for you."

"Fabian, what are you talking about? What do you mean you'll come for me?"

"Nora, I don't have time, I have to leave. Just trust me."

With a sad smile that showed appreciation, she slipped on her dress and walked toward the door.

Fabian, who was opening the door, noticed from the corner of his eye that the blinds were up just as he heard the loud thump that shook the floor.

He turned around and looked at the window that displayed a clean bullet hole. He made to start running, but stopped when he saw Nora lying on the floor with blood pooling around her head.

Immediately, Fabian dove over her body and began dragging it away from the window. He turned her around and caressed her head.

"No...no...no..." he whimpered.

Seeing the shadow of the gunman walk away, he reached for his own gun and approached the window, crying out, "Motherfucker!"

He returned to Nora's body, hyperventilating as he told himself, "These motherfuckers are going to pay."

With no other option, he grabbed the cash that was clinched in her hand, placed it back in his duffel bag, kissed her on the lips and left the apartment.

Fabian fearlessly walked down the stairs, the duffel bag over his shoulder, and his pistol in his hand. Without caution, he walked out of the building, opened the trunk of his father's car and drove away to pick up his brothers and Frankie.

Chapter IV

Just A Few Things

Jumping several rooftops proved to be physically challenging for Sebastian, who was already hurt from the previous getaway. He, Frankie and Khan reached their destination at the neighborhood Latin Club on California Avenue, undetectably blending in with the club patrons who were on the rooftop patio, immorally socializing.

The three amigos calmly walked through the rooftop entrance to avoid being noticed by anyone employed by

Avner. Inconspicuous to the unacquainted eye, they made their way down the stairs and straight into the club's kitchen, which led them to the club's main office. The office belonged to the club's owner and longtime associate of Avner, Omar Santana.

"We're here to see Omar," Sebastian said to the bouncer, who showed no signs of moving from the door.

"Omar will see you when he feels like seeing you."

"Perhaps I didn't make myself clear. I said we're here to see Omar, you steroid-junkie motherfucker," Sebastian said, stepping up face-to-face with the bouncer.

"Sebastian, we need to deal with this a little more calmly," Khan nervously advised.

"No, he understands perfectly," Sebastian said to Khan, who did not realize Sebastian had his .45 pointed at the bouncer's crotch. "Isn't that right, Hercules?"

"So, what? You're going to shoot me in front of everyone?" the bouncer arrogantly questioned him.

"Shit, you're right, everyone will hear me blow your dick off. Frankie!" Sebastian yelled out. He moved out of the way so Frankie could walk toward the bouncer, displaying his .45 with a silencer attached to it, ready to shoot.

"Okay, okay!" the bouncer responded, now nervous.

"Don't ever challenge me again, you stupid fuck," Sebastian said to him. He whacked the bouncer in the head with his pistol, sending him crashing to the floor and allowing them to open the door.

"Whoa!" Frankie yelled out. They entered the office and witnessed Omar snorting coke off a large-breasted woman.

Omar angrily stared at his bouncer as he wiped his nose clean, and allowed his female delicacy to quickly dress and exit the office.

"Fuck me, did you see the tits on that girl?" Frankie asked Sebastian, patting him on the shoulder.

"Is there something you boys need?" Omar asked, caught off guard. "In case you guys haven't noticed, I'm a little busy right now."

"Busy? Yeah, I guess that's certainly one way of looking at it," Frankie responded, pointing at the bouncer to have a seat on the sofa.

"Khan, I've known you and your brothers for a real long time. I've done business with you guys for some time now and this is how you show gratitude for our friendship?" Omar asked as he sat down behind his desk and lit up a cigarette.

"We're not here to rob you, and we're not here to disrespect you in any way."

"Not here to disrespect me? Really?" Omar responded, glancing at Frankie who had his gun pointed at the bouncer's head.

"We actually need your help," Khan calmly explained.

"I wouldn't call it that," Sebastian cut in.

"Sebastian, shut the fuck up and let me handle this," Khan snapped.

"Oh, so now you're handling this?" Sebastian asked, his sarcasm obvious.

"Well, I negotiate a lot better than you."

"Really, Khan?"

"Is there something that you need from me?" Omar intervened, annoyed.

"We need guns, ammo, those untraceable cell phones and a car," Khan asked.

"What the fuck? Do I look like a one-stop shop, here?" Omar answered with a smirk.

"We've always looked out for each other," Sebastian added.

"Yes, we have. But never have I come over to your joint, pointed a gun and demanded shit like this. Truthfully, I find it insulting."

"We mean no disrespect," Khan said.

"You mean no disrespect?" Omar demanded.

"Omar, what my brother is trying to say is that we know you're under Avvi's payroll, and we couldn't take any chances," Sebastian explained as he placed his pistol in its holster.

"What the fuck did you guys do?" Omar apprehensively asked. "Do I need to start looking over my shoulder?"

"Omar, listen to me. You're okay, I guess."

"You guess? What the fuck does that mean, Sebastian?"

"What it means is that we came here, held you at gunpoint and took what we needed. It covers your ass."

"You're good, Omar," Khan tried to assure him.

"Fuck you, you fucking chink. And fuck you, Sebastian," Omar yelled. He was starting to realize that his operation, and potentially his friendship with Avner Levine, was jeopardized.

"And let me explain something to you wannabe, wise-guy cocksuckers: I am not under Avner's payroll. I contribute to it weekly, you fucking douchebags!"

"Omar, calm down."

"Calm down? Calm down? Let me educate you dumb motherfuckers on something. Avner Levine owns this neighborhood. He has owned it before any of us were able to do business around here. So fuck you, fuck you and FUCK YOU, Frankie. Don't think I forgot about you!"

"What the fuck are you smiling at?" Frankie asked the bouncer, who was indeed smiling at them.

"I'm smiling at three soon-to-be-dead dumb motherfuckers."

"Oh yeah, dead? I'll show you dead," Frankie yelled, pointing his pistol and ready to shoot the bouncer.

"Frankie! We need to remain focused here," Khan pleaded with him.

"Look, all we need is those three things and we're out of here for a long time, until we can straighten out this misunderstanding," Khan said to Omar.

"Allow me to explain to you dumb fucks my thoughts about your sad state of affairs. And please, don't get me wrong, but I really don't give a shit about what you consider is a misunderstanding between Mr. Levine and you douchebags. But let's make one thing clear here: when that crazy Jew fuck henchmen of Levine's—what's his fucking name?" Omar asked his bouncer as he snapped his finger. "I could never say his name because it hurts my throat."

"Heiman," the bouncer replied.

"Yeah, whatever he said—when he comes asking for you guys, fellas, I have no other choice but to tell him, do you understand me? This is no fucking joke here."

"Omar, I know a few things about you and a certain family member of Mr. Levine that can change the nature of the relationship between the two of you. Do you understand me?" Sebastian asked him, dismayed.

"That was a long time ago," Omar countered. "Besides, you knowing about this for so long, and now wanting to reveal this information, isn't going to work out for you."

"Sebastian, what the hell are you talking about?" Frankie asked, genuinely curious.

"Do you remember Avvi's niece Allona?"

"Which one? The young girl whose bat mitzvah we went to several years ago?" Frankie said, trying to remember her face and the event.

"Yup. Well, Mr. Soon-to-give-us-what-we're-asking-for here was banging that like a broken screen door in the wind when she was barely sixteen years old."

"No one can prove that," Omar said, trying to dismiss the accusation.

"Like hell I can't," Sebastian fired back. "You were like, what, thirty-something years old at the time?"

"Oh yeah, I remember her now. The girl with the schnoz and the tits," Frankie added as he started remembering her. "Dude, doesn't she have a child, like out of wedlock?"

"Almost Spanish looking if you ask me," Sebastian replied.

Khan, who couldn't believe what he was listening to, covered his mouth and shook his head. He stared at Omar, who now displayed a shamefaced look.

"You motherfuckers!" Omar angrily yelled.

"Who the hell are you calling a motherfucker, you cynical, pedophile son-of-a-bitch!" Sebastian immediately fired back.

With a deep inhale and exhale, Omar knew that his situation, just like theirs, had taken a turn for the worst. He had no other choice but to comply with their demands.

"What the fuck do you hijo de putas want?"

"We want the money you owe us, some firepower, cell phones, and a vehicle to be picked up at a later time."

"I don't owe you money. I pay off Mr. Levine, not you guys."

"No, you stupid Ecuadorian son-of-a-bitch!" Frankie angrily fired back. "You owe us for all the stupid little shit you never wanted to take care of yourself, because you refused to squeeze a trigger."

"I paid Avner for those services."

"Yes, you did, but it was us who put the work in," Frankie responded.

"Well perhaps you should have chosen a different profession," Omar replied sarcastically.

"You're right, and I'll consider changing it once I'm done with you," Frankie responded, pointing his pistol at Omar.

"Guys, chill the fuck out. We still need to get the hell out of here, and get out of here alive," Khan shouted, aggravated with the turn of events.

"Are you going to help us or not?" Sebastian asked Omar.

"All I have is forty thousand in cash, a couple of AK's, several M4's, about three M67 fragmentation grenades, colored smoke grenades, and a shitload of ammo."

"What the fuck, Omar? Are you preparing for war?" Khan asked him, shocked.

"Well, considering the type of business we're involved in, it's not like we're all in this together, looking out for one another. Besides, most of this stuff is illegal to own, so have at it," Omar eagerly said.

"What about a car?" Sebastian asked.

"I have a cousin who is married to a yahoo in Clinton County Iowa. He owns a shop up there and has done business for me. I'll give him a call and have him set you up. Is there anything else you want to fuck me over with?"

"As a matter of fact, there is. We need those untraceable phones. At least four," Sebastian asked as he looked out the window that faced the dance floor.

"Shit, you guys really fucked up, didn't you?" Omar said to them, opening up his safe to take out the cash.

"Avvi was shot. I don't know if he made it," Khan told him, showing signs of being nervous.

Omar stopped for a second to actually think about the situation. He did not want to know what had happened, because the less a person knew in this business, the better off they were.

"I can assure you, we had nothing to with it," Khan said to him.

"Yeah, okay Khan, whatever you say," Omar replied. "You got what you needed and now you can all do me a favor and just get the fuck out of my club."

None of them responded to Omar. They knew, had the situation been the other way around, Omar would have probably ended up dead.

"Do you think Fabian's back?" Khan asked, placing four, ten thousand dollars stacks in his specially-modified money belt.

"He should be, however, walking out the front isn't a good idea," Sebastian explained as he grabbed a large duffel bag filled with weapons.

"Shit, I'm getting really tired of climbing and jumping fucking rooftops," said Frankie, placing his gun in its holster.

"Go ahead, big boy. Now is the time for you to act like a fucking frog and leap!" he said to Omar's bouncer in a challenging manner.

"Just take your fucking money, the guns and get the fuck out!" Omar yelled. He realized that Frankie was on edge and needed to get frustration out of his system.

"Frankie, chill out. We're almost done and will be leaving soon," Khan tried to calm him down. Frankie's aggressive, challenging manner made him nervous.

"Are we ready?" Sebastian asked the two.

"Omar, when this is over, we'll return everything," Khan gratefully said to him.

"When this is over? When this is over I can assure you—"

Bravado Brothers

But before Omar's bouncer was able to finish his threatening response, blood splattered on Omar, Sebastian and Khan's faces.

"Frankie, what the fuck!" Sebastian yelled out as he cleared the blood from his eyes.

Omar's bouncer was on his knees, evaluating the palm of his hand. He saw that two of his fingers were shot off and let out a thunderous, painful scream that ignited a horrifying feeling in Omar, Khan, and Sebastian.

"Go ahead, you stupid motherfucker. Point your finger at me one more motherfucking time, and I promise that your motherfucking day will get a lot worse," Frankie screamed. "As a matter of fact, point your fucking other hand at any of us, and see what the fuck happens next!"

"What the fuck is wrong with you? Did you have to shoot the idiot's fucking fingers off?" Khan frenetically shouted.

"FRANKIE!" Sebastian yelled out in order to restore order.

"You motherfuckers, get the fuck out of my club...NOW!" Omar ordered angrily.

"Fucking crying little bitch!" Frankie yelled at the bouncer as he placed his pistol into the holster again and walked out the door, heading toward the roof.

Sebastian and Khan could only stare at Omar's reaction to his bouncer's finger being shot off before walking off. They remained vigilant to their surroundings as they carefully exited out.

"Omar, what am I going to do?" his bouncer asked, the pain obvious in his voice.

"I'll tell you what you can do: you can shut the fuck up the next time a homicidal maniac has a gun pointed at you, you stupid motherfucker," Omar yelled back and aggressively slapped him in the head.

"Frankie, did you really have to shoot his finger off?" Sebastian laughingly asked him as they made their way up the stairs and exited out the rooftop lounge.

Frankie, however, who was too upset to respond to him. He marched over to a fire escape ladder that led onto a smaller rooftop below. Without judging any distance between buildings, without uttering a word, he jumped from building to building.

Khan and Sebastian looked at each other in total shock, both of them subconsciously grateful that Frankie was on their side.

"Oh well, let's make this great escape happen," Sebastian said to Khan. He slowly and carefully climbed down the ladder and hesitantly crossed over multiple rooftops to catch up with Frankie, who was already quietly waiting for Fabian to arrive at their darkened parking lot rendezvous point.

"Sebastian, Frankie isn't right," Khan whispered.

"What do you mean?"

"I mean, look at him just staring with that cynical gaze."

"Khan, right about now we need that crazy unexplainable man to keep us safe."

Just as Khan was about to reply, he saw his younger brother Fabian inexpressively drive into the parking lot. Without looking, Fabian stopped and popped the trunk of the car, lighting up a cigarette in the process.

"Ah, fuck," Sebastian whispered to Khan as he passed Fabian and headed toward the trunk.

Khan immediately knew that something had gone wrong with Fabian. He dropped his head down, took a deep breath, and mentally accepted shit was about to go south.

"Hey, Fabe, what's up?" Khan asked him as he approached the car. However, when he looked at Fabian's hands which were resting on the steering wheel, he noticed the dried up blood smeared on the side of his palm. It immediately sent a rushing chill throughout Khan's body.

"Hey, little bro, why don't you scoot over and let me drive? I have a lot on my mind and the driving will help me think and make sense of things," Khan said to him.

Fabian did not even question Khan. He opened the car door and, without saying a word, jumped in the back seat, taking deep puffs from his cigarette.

"So, you're smoking now?" Khan asked. He knew that his younger brother did not smoke.

Fabian did not even look at his brother. Instead, he leaned his head back, inhaled another deep drag from his cigarette, closed his eyes and did not utter a word.

With a staunch walk that was menacing in nature, Frankie, the gang's unofficial enforcer, opened the passenger side door. Not saying a word, he sat next to his childhood best friend.

Khan immediately looked at Sebastian to get a visual confirmation that would assure him everything was going to be alright; but he felt uneasy when Sebastian lifted both his eyebrows, indicating that he did not know what to make of Fabian and Frankie's behaviors.

"So, where to now?" Khan asked Sebastian.

"Well, this business card that Omar left in the bag says his cousin's husband's shop is in Clinton County. It's about a two, two and a half hour trip. So let's go I-290 straight out of Chicago and take it to I-88, which will hopefully lead us safely to this location," Sebastian replied.

"Do you think Omar will screw us over once we get there?" Khan asked.

Sebastian lowered the visor down to look in the mirror and watched both Fabian and Frankie. "I don't think Omar wants to be part of any of this; especially with us. I think we'll be alright. But before we make contact with these folks, we'll scout the place out."

"Alright. Iowa or bust," Khan said as he placed the car in drive and peeled away.

Chapter V

Venomous

"Alright guys, it's been over an hour that we've been on the road and not once has anyone said a word," Khan commented to the group.

"You know, that is some sick shit you have going on with yourself. Why don't you just go to a doctor?" Sebastian asked Khan.

"What the hell are you talking about?" Khan replied. He looked in the rearview mirror at Frankie, who was paying close attention to Sebastian's comment.

"What, you don't think any of us have noticed you switching your ass from left to right for over an hour now? Or in the past for that matter?" Sebastian replied.

Khan, who was clearly showing signs of becoming agitated, remained quiet, refusing to comment on his inexplicable condition he had been suffering from for well over five years now.

"What are you talking about?" Frankie asked, breaking his silence.

"Oh, Khan here has a problem keeping his asshole clean," Fabian joined in, breaking his silence as well.

"Keeping his asshole clean?" Frankie asked, his curiosity piqued.

"Yup. He has to go to the bathroom to wipe his ass at least three to four times a day—and that's without having taken a shit," Sebastian explained as he lit up a cigarette.

"Fuck you and fuck you, you fucking ass-wipes," Khan shouted, aggravated.

"You have a lot of nerve, man, calling us an ass-wipe when it's your asshole that is uncontrollably discharging shit," Fabian tells him with a laugh.

"Are you fucking serious? I mean, I've known you guys all my life, and this is the first time I have ever heard of this," Frankie said to them with disgust in his voice. "Are you not wiping your ass thoroughly?"

"You fucking cocksuckers haven't said a word for well over an hour because of your emotional issues and now you want to talk about my shit and ass?" Khan snapped.

"Do you need to pull over at one of these rest stops so that you can wipe your ass?"

With a frustrating sigh that exhibited defeat, Khan, who refused to answer Sebastian's suggestion, grabbed his cigarette box and lighter from the dashboard and placed a cigarette in his lips. As he went to light it, he accidentally dropped the lighter.

"I got it!" Khan yelled in annoyance at Sebastian, who was laughing at him while trying to help him retrieve the lighter that fell underneath the car seat.

"What the hell is this?" Khan asked, now curious as he tried making out what he had grabbed from under the seat.

His brain took a few seconds to register what it was. Then, with a high pitch scream that startled the dead and all life forces surrounding them, Khan lost control of the vehicle, veered off the road and spun uncontrollably into a cornfield.

Fabian, Sebastian, and Frankie did not have the reactionary ability to brace for any potential impact. They were left immobile by the gravitational force from the car spinning under the moonlight and stars' spirals.

The car came to a rocking, side-to-side stop that disrupted all of their equilibriums. Khan, who was almost hyperventilating, held his palm open as he stared at an eyeball.

"What the hell is this? Why am I holding an eyeball?" Khan asked, doing everything in his power to not puke.

"Oh shit. That must be Lorenzo's eye ball," Frankie answered while chuckling at Khan's reaction.

"His fucking eyeball? Is this fucking amusing to you Frankie?" Khan yelled out frantically.

"Shit, now that I think about it, wasn't that Guinea fucker missing his eyes?" Sebastian recalled.

"We're fucked aren't we?" Khan whispered as he tossed the eyeball into the cornfield. "I can't do this Sebastian. I can't go out there and hide like an escaped prisoner."

"Khan, we're in the middle of fucking nowhere. I mean, I don't even know where we're at," Sebastian replied, getting frustrated. "So the last thing I want to hear is that you can't do this. Now, where the fuck are we?"

"We're in Dixon?" Fabian blurted out.

"How the hell do you know that?" Sebastian asked him.

"Because right before Mr. Corn Maze here lost control and veered off the road—"

"I got your fucking corn maze right here, motherfucker!" Khan yelled out as he leaped over the seat to attack his younger brother.

"Whoa, whoa, whoa," they all yelled while trying to stop Khan from advancing his assault.

"You need to chill the fuck out, Khan," Sebastian yelled, trying to maintain his composure. "And you, stop being a wise ass," he barked at Fabian, who had a smirk on his face.

"We are by no means out of the woods yet…Fabian, shut the hell up!" Sebastian interjected, stopping him from making a sarcastic remark which would send Khan charging at him again.

"Look, let's slowly drive out of here and get to this meeting point in Clinton, so that we can get to this pigs in a blanket place."

"Pig's Eye Landing," Frankie corrected Sebastian.

"Whatever. Let's just get the hell out of here."

"You boys aren't going anywhere," a farmer standing just outside their car calmly said, racking his shotgun. "Unless you're my migrant workers ready to get an early start at picking the corn on my field, then you are, what many would consider, fucked for trespassing."

"No sir, we are not migrant workers. We just veered off the road and we will be on our way out now," Sebastian cautiously replied.

"Well, none of that matters at this point, so do me a favor and slowly step out of the car, one at a time."

Frankie and Fabian had slowly reached into their pockets to get a hold of their guns. They were readying themselves to shoot their way out, but froze in movement when the farmer quickly walked behind them to conceal his location.

Fabian slightly turned toward Frankie to validate the farmer's cunningness and smiled at the tactical move. It was a move his father relentlessly preached to the boys for many years: "Keep your enemy mentally and physically off balance."

"I don't know what you're up to, but we will see if the police can accommodate you boys," the farmer said.

After several seconds of uneasy silence, Fabian, who refused to deal with any kind of law enforcement outside of Chicago, decided to take a chance, and swiftly turned around and pulled the trigger four times.

"Fabian, are you crazy?" Sebastian yelled, startled by the sudden gunfire.

"He had to take him out, Sebastian," Frankie said, approving of Fabian's decision.

"Shit, Sebastian, this is not good," Khan mumbled as he rubbed his face in disbelief.

Frankie and Fabian were the first to jump out of the car, and immediately walked over to the body with their guns drawn and pointed at the farmer.

"Son of a bitch, is he still breathing?" Frankie asked them in astonishment.

"I'm a good fucking shot...what can I say?" Fabian replied.

"Let's drag him to the front of the car near the lights," Frankie said, glancing at Khan and Sebastian, both of whom were still in the car in a state of shock.

"Hey guys, in case you haven't noticed, this fat fuck is well over three hundred pounds. So, before you go into a state of panic, can you give us a hand here?" Frankie sarcastically requested to the two brothers.

The four of them each grabbed a limb and dragged the body to the front of the car. Khan tilted his head to analyze the body and noticed that there was no blood.

"Guys, why isn't there any blood?" Khan asked.

"What do you mean?" Fabian questioned as he struggled to drag the body.

"I mean, there isn't any blood. I thought you shot the fat fuck four times?" Khan said.

"I did."

Then, for the second time in one night, Khan let out a high pitch scream that would shatter a beer mug and dropped their casualty before leaping into the car.

Fabian, Sebastian, and Frankie also released their hold of the body and immediately leaped onto the hood of the car. They looked down at the farmer's body, where there was now a large, southern copperhead snake slithering away from, heading out into the moonlit cornfields.

Frankie noticed that the farmer's ankle was starting to swell, and jumped off the hood of the car. He immediately lifted the farmer's pants leg to confirm his suspicion.

"What are you looking at?" Sebastian whispered.

"Sebastian, there is absolutely no one around us and snakes can't hear you whisper."

"Just answer the question, you fucking asshole," Sebastian whispered louder.

"Well, Khan's theory might be correct, because there are no bullet holes, therefore no blood. There is, however, what I believe is a nasty snake bite."

"What do you mean a snake bite?" Khan asked.

"Well, usually, a farmer will wear boots when they're out in the fields working; however, this sorry sack of shit is wearing sandals. Probably because he heard Madame

Butterfly here scream like a bitch, came out after a hard day's work to investigate and, as a result, got bit."

Fabian looked at Khan and started laughing at him.

"What the hell are you laughing at Mr. 'I'm a good fucking shot...what can I say'," Khan shouted. "You didn't hit your fucking target from a close range."

"Screw you, you slant-eyed son of a bitch," Fabian shouted to Khan as the two were backed away from each other by Frankie and Sebastian.

"Calm down!" Sebastian yelled. He realized that at any given moment their situation could get even worst.

"This is not good. We need to do something, and something quick," Frankie insisted. He started looking around his surroundings to see if anyone was coming to search for the farmer.

"Well, we don't need him for anything, so let's drag this snake-bit, three hundred pound fucker into the fields. It should buy us several hours before anyone even notices."

"Yeah, go ahead Fabe. I'm sure you can handle this one," Khan said sarcastically to his younger brother, walking to the driver's side of the car and sitting down.

"Ah, I don't know about that one," Frankie said, jumping in the back seat.

Fabian, who decided to give into the banter, looked one last time to see if he could find at least a grazing from the bullets anywhere around the farmer's body.

"Let's go, Fabe. It's pointless," Sebastian told his kid brother.

"Shit!" Fabian cursed out into the moonlit cornfields.

Chapter VI

Clinton

"Man, it's really fucking dark out here," said Khan as he placed the car in park behind an unattended warehouse and looked around their surroundings.

"Look, this auto shop, according to what Omar wrote down, is right around the corner. Frankie and I will walk around to make sure everything is clear," said Sebastian.

"Why you and Frankie? Why can't we all go?" Khan asked, clearly irked.

"Well, no offense, but having a chink walking around these streets in Middle America may make things look suspicious," Sebastian explained.

"First of all, I'm Vietnamese, you stupid spic-fuck; and secondly, what makes you think that two Hispanic guys walking around, what you call Middle America, wouldn't raise any suspicion?

"I'm half Polish, you son of a bitch!" Frankie fired back.

"Oh yeah, that really changes everything. What was I thinking?" Khan sarcastically replied.

"Oh my god, fine. I didn't think you were going to get your panties in a wad," Sebastian conceded. "I tell you what: you and Frankie go in one direction, and Fabian and I will go in another. We'll meet up in the back to make sure we're not walking into an ambush."

"Fine," Khan agreed as he looked at his watch.

Per Sebastian's plan, they walked toward their location in two separate groups from opposite directions. Sebastian and Fabian were the first to arrive behind the auto shop, which was nestled in the middle of the street. It seemed free of any local activity, but that sentiment, as reassuring as it should have been, did not feel welcoming. Most criminals suffered from a mistrust of calm surroundings.

"Sebastian, I'm going to hit the back real quick to see if anyone is inside," said Fabian, hoping to get the jump on any unexpected activity.

"Alright, watch your six and don't pull it out unless you have to. Do you understand me, Fabe?"

"Yes."

Bravado Brothers

Worried about Fabian's combative behavior, Sebastian looked on as his younger brother slowly walked toward the back of the auto shop. Fabian immediately scanned his surroundings to identify anything unusual.

"Where the hell are Khan and Frankie?" Sebastian asked himself. He felt they were taking a long time to reach the auto shop, especially considering they left before him and Fabian.

Sebastian searched inside his pocket, removed a pack of cigarettes and angled his head down for several seconds to look for his lighter. He felt a presence come behind him, but ignored it, believing it was Fabian.

"There's no smoking in the shop, son," a gravelly-voiced man said to him from behind.

Sebastian sensed that the voice possessed an authoritarian demeanor. Instinctively, he looked at the boots and knew that the man wearing them was not a shop owner, but law enforcement.

"Ok, son, slowly turn around. Please do yourself a favor, and make no sudden moves," he instructed Sebastian.

Based on the Midwest accent and drawn-out speech, Sebastian knew that there wasn't going to be any room for compromise for a Chicagoan. In this part of the country, the only excitement law enforcement was accustomed to, was watching corn grow.

"Is there a problem, sir?"

With a raspy chuckle, the man took several steps backward and revealed himself as a deputy sheriff. He smiled at Sebastian as he pointed his gun at him. "Now when was the last time you ever addressed anyone with 'sir'?"

Sebastian refused to give into the deputy's prodding, for he knew that this was not going to end with a warning. He returned the smile and said, "So, where are we going?"

"We're going to where you were originally heading to, so Andale," he ordered Sebastian, waving his gun at him.

As the deputy and Sebastian walked into the secluded lot that stored salvaged vehicles, Sebastian was relieved to see that his brother was okay. He quickly became discouraged when he saw Khan and Frankie being held at gunpoint.

"I have to admit, your partner here could have blended in with the locals, but him walking around with the chink, well that's an entirely different story," the deputy sheriff pointed out, forcing Sebastian, Fabian, and Frankie to stare at Khan.

"So, what do you want?" asked Khan, refusing to look at his brothers and friend.

"It's not him you need to be asking that to, it's me," a burly, six foot four hillbilly said to Khan. "So, which one of you has the sissy name of Sebastian?" he asked the four.

"That would be me."

With a laughter that wheezed from years of heavy smoking, the mammoth of a man pulled out a seat to rest his body, lit up a cigarette, cocked his head back and blew out the smoke with a hard exhale.

"Bob, you know you're not supposed to be lighting that in here," the deputy sheriff said to him.

"Will you hush and let me deal with the situation at hand," Bob replied back, never losing focus on Sebastian. "So, it was brought to my attention that I am to assist you wetbacks with a vehicle. However, here's the problem: there's a hefty reward for the four of you, and, quite frankly, I really don't give a shit what you boys are accused of. I can assure you that money will make anyone think differently."

Bob's remarks to Sebastian brought to light for the first time what the bounty on their heads was.

"Did Omar explain to you who we are?" Sebastian asked him as he watched several men enter the auto shop and begin to tie up Khan, Frankie, and Fabian.

"Well, this is the other thing: I never really liked Omar. Yes, we've worked together and I'm married to his cousin, but he is scum of the earth and I couldn't care less what he thinks or is asking for. Comprende?"

Sebastian closed his eyes to avoid the smoke that was being intentionally blown directly at his face. He became infuriated as he watched his three allies get tied up and become redeemable pawns for an act they were never responsible for.

"I do have one question—what on earth are you guys doing with a chink?" Bob asked Sebastian, continuing to blow smoke directly into his face.

"Fuck you, you cow fucking, sibling raping, fat motherfucker!" Khan shouted.

"Well, well, well, listen to the mouth on Mr. La Choy here," the grizzly-sized auto shop owner commented, standing up and extinguishing his cigarette. "Don't take it personally, little man, because in the end, whether you're a yellow monkey or a river nigger, to me, you fuckers serve no purpose in this world. So, believe me when I tell you all that I couldn't give two flying rat asses what these Jew fucks want with you, as long as I get my money."

With their hands bound to a hydraulic car lift and their fates in the hands of a radical yahoo salivating at the very idea of a big payday, Sebastian, Khan, Fabian, and Frankie could only stare at each other in astonishment as their bounty hunter walked away to receive a phone call.

"Don't worry, my amigos. This will all be over real soon," the deputy sheriff taunted.

"Alright, change of plans. They only want the Fabian fellow, not the rest of them. And the best part? Same price!" the shop owner contentedly explained to the deputy sheriff.

"What about the others? Do we let them go?"

"Fuck no, they already know who we are. Just get rid of them and take them to the basement. I have to take Paco back to that cesspool they call Chicago and get my money," he explained.

Sebastian watched helplessly as his kid brother got dragged away by a man they only knew as Bob and placed in the back of an SUV. He began to plead with the deputy sheriff, who smiled at the very idea of taking them to the basement to finish them off.

"Whatever they offered you, we can pay you twice the amount if you just let us go. You have my word on that—"

Mid-negotiation, Sebastian was viciously punched in the face by the deputy sheriff to stop him from speaking.

"You shut the fuck up and take it like a man, you fucking cockroach spic motherfucker!" the deputy sheriff yelled at

Sebastian. "Release him. He's the first one to go down," he ordered a shop worker, who was there to assist.

Before the shop worker could do as he was told, Khan, who had always been known for having small wrists and hands, managed to slip out of the reef knot that was poorly applied. He grabbed a blowtorch propane cylinder from a workstation and used it to crack open the skull of the shop attendant.

The deputy was unable to reach for his pistol quickly enough to stop Khan's attack, so he leaped at Khan to remove the cylinder from his hands, but was too late. Khan was already prepared to counterattack and struck the officer behind the ear, causing him to collapse on the shop floor. He continuously struck the deputy sheriff until he was exhausted from the hostile attack.

"Fuck, Khan, I didn't think you had it in you," Frankie gratefully said to him, as he watched Khan pant profusely.

Having never viciously attacked or killed anyone before, as Khan wiped the blood that covered his eyes and mouth with his sleeve, he immediately threw up when he started spitting out fragments of bone and skin from his mouth.

"Khan...Khan..." Frankie yelled, snapping Khan back to reality. "Get me out of this shit, we need to get Fabian."

"What the hell have I done?" Khan screamed hysterically.

We can talk about this over coffee if you like, but right now you need to untie me."

"What have I done?" Khan cried out again, weeping.

"What you did was help save our asses, Khan. Now hurry the fuck up!" Frankie urged him, realizing that time was running out.

Khan freed Frankie from his bondage, and Frankie immediately ran to free Sebastian, who looked unstable.

"Goodness, Khan, you worry me sometimes," Frankie said. "Now, listen to me: go clean yourself up, change clothes if you can, and get past this because we're going to get the hell out of here."

As Frankie helped Sebastian stabilize and talked some sense into Khan, he heard the entrance door open and close. "Shit someone is coming, get down," Frankie ordered the two brothers in a whisper.

"Hey Craig, I left my travel bag in my office," Bob yelled out.

"Finally, a name to the scumbag deputy," Frankie thought to himself.

"Craig, you there? Son of a bitch!" Bob screamed as he saw the pool of blood and brain matter on the garage floor.

"I got the name of the douchebag laying on the floor, but I never got yours—I mean, there's no way your name is Bob," Frankie yelled out as he removed the service weapon from the dead deputy and pointed it directly at the shop owner.

"You're a dead son of a bitch!"

"You know, I have been in many parts of this great country of ours, and, like my brothers here, I have served my country proudly. As a result, I've met a lot of people. But never have I ever met a person named 'you're a dead son of a bitch'," Frankie sarcastically replied, pointing the pistol at Bob's head.

Then, as the shop owner was about to talk, Sebastian aggressively kicked him behind the leg, bringing him down to his knees.

"Here's the fat fuck's wallet," Khan said to Frankie.

"Well, well, well, what do we have here? Earl Lester White," Frankie commented as he looked at the driver's license. "Yup, that's about right, wouldn't you say there, Sebastian?"

"Well listen up, Earl, or whatever they call you. Shit's not looking good for you right about now," Sebastian said to him as he patted him on the back. "The way I see it, all of this could have been avoided, and we would have been on our merry way. But no, you chose differently. Truthfully, I'm really not shocked."

"Ah, guys, you need to see this shit," Khan said in disbelief.

"Whatcha got?" Frankie asked, walking over toward the small office where Khan was standing. "Oh shit. Sebastian, you need to come take a look at this."

"What is it?" Sebastian asked, never losing focus on Earl.

Then, like a tomb raider discovering treasure, Frankie wheeled out a dolly piled with three creates, each filled with dynamite.

"Now you leave that alone, that's for my rock quarry, you—"

"Damn, Sebastian, you really knocked him the fuck out," Frankie said, laughing as he watched Earl fall face first onto the concrete floor after Sebastian struck him behind the head with a wrench. "Shit, we forgot about Fabe," he realized out loud, as he looked out the window.

"What about the others?" Khan questioned.

"I think Mr. Earl here prematurely sent them home thinking he was in the clear," Frankie replied. He had a clear view of the car and noticed that no one was in the car or waiting outside.

"Well, go get him," Sebastian said, casting glances between the box filled with dynamite and Earl's crumpled body.

* *

"Look, he's coming around," Khan shouted out as he added the finishing touches of duct taping several sticks of dynamite around Earl's upper body. He had been an explosive ordnance disposal specialist in the Army.

"Rise and shine, big boy," Fabian said to the shop owner. "It's been well over an hour since you've been out. You really must have been tired, or my brother really knocked you out bad."

"Fuck you."

"Wow, aside from having a massive big gut, you have some big balls, Earl. To look at the man who is about to light your ass up straight to hell and say 'fuck you' takes a special kind of human. I admire that," Frankie said to him with a smile.

"Fabe, it's time to head out," Sebastian said to his younger brother as he realized Fabian was staring at Earl with tunnel vision.

"You know, money makes a person do stupid shit. I offered your partner there, Mr. No-head, more money and he, just like you, didn't take it," Frankie continued bantering. "Truth be told, that one is going to eat me up when we drive away with the vehicle you provided for us; or should I say, the one we're taking from you."

"You fucking corn-picking field niggers ain't got the balls."

"What exactly is that anyway? Is that some derogatory Mexican joke or something? Were we supposed to be offended?" Fabian interrogated him.

"Enough, Fabe, let's go," Sebastian said. He was starting to get nervous with all the gas, dynamite and his hothead brother.

"You know what, you're not worth the bullet," Frankie said to Earl. "I'd rather slowly watch your demise than just shoot you in the head. Do you understand me, Earl?"

"I look in your eyes and I see pussy written all over them," Earl said, showing no signs of fear.

"Frankie, he's fucking with you. Don't fall for that shit," Khan cautioned Frankie as he finished setting up to activate the dynamite.

"So? What's the deal?" Sebastian asked Khan.

"Well, we'll have about twenty minutes to get the hell out of dodge before this place lights up the neighborhood," Khan responded.

"Is that enough time?"

"Yeah, we should be on the highway by the time this place lights up," Khan assured him.

"Fabian, I know this fat fuck was going to trade you in, but you're still alive and we're all together. So forget about this possum-eating motherfucker, and let's get the hell out," Frankie said. "Besides, there will be no evidence and no bodies to identify."

Fabian was still upset about the whole ordeal. He looked at Earl's shop worker, wrapped around the shop owner's neck, and a near-headless deputy sheriff, used as Earl's footrest. After deliberating, Fabian conceded,

"Fine, let's go."

The four looked around at their surroundings and became overwhelmed with apprehension. They were also appreciative that they accomplished what they came out to Clinton for, despite having hit a few roadblocks.

"So what are we going to do with the old man's car?" Khan asked.

"There's a high school not far from here. Let's drop it off there for the time being, and when it's safe to return we'll come for it," Frankie suggested.

"You don't think the locals will mess with it?" Khan asked.

"Khan, we're in bumfuck Iowa. The only excitement these folks are going to get is the explosion that's going to take place real soon," Sebastian explained to him.

Sebastian jumped in his old man's car and began to drive away, with the other three following him in their newly acquired getaway car. Sebastian parked the old car, hopped in with his brothers and friend and started driving away toward Minnesota.

As they took off down the road, Fabian leaned his head back and looked at his watch. Realizing that they had been driving for more than thirty minutes, Fabian became a little nervous. He remembered Khan mentioning it would take about twenty minutes for the bomb to detonate.

"Khan, you do realize that it has been more than—"

"Shh," Khans interrupted Fabian, annoyed that his craftwork was being questioned.

Then, from a great distance away, there was a faint explosion sound and a small, fiery mushroom rose into the air. Khan, who was driving, looked at Fabian from the rearview mirror without saying a word.

"Well *excuuuse* me," Fabian mumbled under his breath before leaning his head back to take a nap.

Chapter VII

Pig's Eye Landing

"So, did we make it to this Pig's Eye Place?" Fabian asked as he woke up from a deep, three-hour long sleep.

"Pig's Eye Landing, you dick," Frankie replied back.

"It's an unusual name for a city," Khan commented as he viewed the scenery zip by him at seventy miles an hour.

"It's actually St. Paul's," Frankie explained, reflecting back to when he was a child and visited his cousins there.

"Your cousin lives there?" Sebastian inquired.

"Many of my Polish ancestors made their home there. It's also where my mother was born. Anyhow, my mom used to send me here as a kid to keep me away from you douchebags, only I'd end up in trouble with my cousin Adam, who we're going to be hanging out with for a few months down here."

Khan, who had forgotten that he was on the run, turned toward Sebastian, who was quietly listening and looking around the towns and cities on I-35.

"Are we going to be good there?" Fabian asked.

"Yeah, he's a good guy. Someone I can trust. Besides, he knows this town and the town knows him, which is a good thing for us," Frankie assured them as he watched the exit signs. "Khan, get off exit 106B. Make a right at the light and, when you get to Seventh Street, find a parking spot near Walnut."

"Is that where your cousin's place is at?"

"Not too far, but first we need to go somewhere and get a drink."

"Sounds like a plan," Khan enthusiastically replied.

They exited the highway after the long, exhausting drive and admired the alluring social scene that introduced an assortment of bars, restaurants, and a sports arena. Sebastian, Khan, and Fabian, who had never visited St. Paul, smiled at one another, as the very idea of opportunities to make money in St. Paul's was encouraging.

"So your family is from these parts?" Sebastian asked.

"From what I've been told throughout the years, when my family came and settled in America back in the mid to late

1800s, many of them were involved in whiskey smuggling and selling it to the soldiers and the Indians. Now, I don't know how much truth there is to that claim, but nevertheless, it's where my family got their start."

"Wait a minute, wait a minute, wait a minute—you mean to tell me that you historically come from a long line of criminals?" Sebastian asked him, curious.

Frankie, who took a few moments to think about this statement, couldn't help but chuckle at Sebastian's comment. "Well, shit, I guess I do."

Frankie looked around and noticed the changes in their surroundings becoming more familiar. He said to the group, "Alright, here we are."

The four stepped out of the vehicle and realized that they were strangers in a strange land. They couldn't help but feel that they were being watched; not by Heiman, or anyone on the hunt for them, but by the locals.

"There's a bar that my cousin hangs out at just a few blocks away. I agreed for all of us to meet him there. But guys, we're not in Chicago, we're not known here and, most importantly, we're not here to make enemies," Frankie explained, directing his comments mostly at Fabian.

"Are you listening to any of this?" Sebastian said to Fabian, who tried avoiding Frankie's comment. "I'm not joking with you, Fabe, this shit is serious!"

"Fine!" Fabian sharply replied.

"Look, I understand that we're not in our environment and this isn't home. But, believe it or not, this place isn't that bad; not to mention, I don't think we'll be running into that Jew fuck bastard, Heiman," Frankie explained to them all.

"Thank you, Frankie. You've been a loyal, lifelong friend and I hope I can repay you someday," Sebastian told him as he gave his best friend a wholehearted embrace.

"Well, don't thank me yet. We're still not out of woods."

"How do I look?" Khan asked, looking at his reflection in the car window glass as he straightened himself up.

"Like a Chinese delivery boy!" Fabian snapped at him as they started walking.

Like desperadoes zoned in on their objective, the four intrepidly walked the composed streets that were now called home for the time being. They all began to admire the amenities and subtle environment.

Sebastian, like a cat tossed in the air and landing on its feet, envisioned the potential of generating a substantial amount of cash in a short period of time by operating illegal numbers and sports gambling. He understood that, although his approach was old school thinking and one that could potentially land them into trouble with the local wise guys, they had to start from the bottom and it was a sure way of profiting from the circumstances.

"This might work," Sebastian thought to himself, looking over at Khan, who he loved as if he was his own biological brother. He appreciated Khan's natural ability of exceptional negotiating; it was, after all, why his former boss Avner used him to conduct business for the family.

As they continued walking the neighborhood streets and scoped out the local action with great detail, Sebastian felt at ease for the first time since their ordeal with Avner. However, that sense of comfort was disrupted when he looked at the reflection of his younger brother Fabian cast in the storefront windows.

Fabian was tall, well-built and never backed down from anyone, along with their childhood best friend and the enforcer of the crew, Frankie. Sebastian knew that, as much as he appreciated their dependability, their tenacious behavior could prove to be disastrous.

"So this cousin of yours, is he a hooligan as well? Or is he a straight shooter just wanting to help out his cousin?" Sebastian asked Frankie as they neared their rendezvous point and he started feeling butterflies in his stomach.

"My cousin Adam reminds me of Red—a real fucking bulldozer, know what I mean?" Frankie responded.

"You mean he's crazier than your spic-polack ass?" Fabian asked him.

"I don't know about all that, but he hustles and he's well known around these parts. I do know that during the winter, which is brutal down here, he's a bouncer in some strip-joint."

"Yeah, that's what's up," Fabian enthusiastically uttered.

"Yup, we might be able to get you some fatties while we're out here," Frankie replied to Fabian right as they entered the bar.

Fabian, who had forgotten about Nora and her unwarranted death up until that point, immediately shut his emotions down as they walked into the local bar to meet up with Frankie's cousin. The atmosphere of the longtime popular establishment and staple in St. Paul's introduced the four to an arousing aroma of fish and chips, mixed drinks, and women's fragrances. It made them feel welcomed.

Many of the patrons, who proudly sported green and white Minnesota Wild hockey jerseys, were all lubing up and preparing themselves for a game that was about to broadcast live.

The barmaids were all top heavy, long-haired, comely woman, crisscrossing each other to attend to their orders. They were visually pleasing, especially to Fabian who considered himself a meat-and-potatoes kind of guy.

"You boys want to be seated in the lounge or find a spot at the bar?" a barmaid asked.

"The lounge will be nice," Sebastian replied, his attention noticeably rapt with her pleasant demeanor, which complemented her Midwestern beauty.

Illuminated by the flat screens that surrounded the wood-covered lounge, the hockey jersey-sporting barmaid, with her piercing eyes and long-flowing hair, turned to show the four to their seating and accidentally bumped into Sebastian.

"Oh, excuse me," she said to Sebastian, who had a fifty dollar bill in his hands.

"Thank you for your hospitality," he replied to her as she grabbed the bill, smiled and walked away.

"Damn, Sebastian, I thought you were going to jam your tongue up her ass," Frankie said to him with a smirk.

"Give me a little time and I will."

Bravado Brothers

"Alright, three pitchers," a short, Spanish-looking barmaid said to them as she placed the pitchers on top of their table, along with five mugs.

"We didn't order this, miss," Khan respectfully said to her.

"No, you didn't—I did," a tall, massive-sized man replied to him.

"Co jest, KuzynemI?" (What's up cousin?)

Frankie and his cousin embraced each other the way two bears wrestle each other out in the wild, catching the attention of patrons socializing in the lounge. Adam, who made Frankie look small, placed a grin on Sebastian, Fabian, and Khan's faces. They knew that if everything worked out according to plan, Adam most certainly was going to be a valuable asset.

"Allow me to introduce you to my brothers at arms: Adam Kowalski. Adam, this is Sebastian Rodriguez, Fabian Rodriguez, and Khan Phan-Rodriguez."

"Khan Phan-Rodriguez? Did they switch you out at birth?" Adam asked with a sarcastic tone.

"Well, no, I was adopted and—" Khan began explaining, but was stopped by Sebastian.

"Khan, he's fucking with you," Sebastian explained.

Khan, who could only stare at Adam as he tried to read his sincerity, smiled at him. He pulled out a Ruger 1911 .45 caliber pistol in one hand while shaking Adam's hand with the other. "You ever make fun of my Puerto Rican culture, I will blow your over-sized Polish head off."

Bravado Brothers

For a few seconds, silence curbed their remarks; then, Khan and Adam embraced.

"Yeah, I can see the Puerto Rican in you...especially with the slanted eyes. My bad, brother," Adam replied, and the four roared with laughter.

"Well, I don't know about you guys, but I need a pint."

Adam began to pour beer into all the mugs. Then, after he poured the last mug, a voluptuous barmaid served five shot glasses filled with Jameson Irish Whiskey.

"Here's to drinking it today and shitting it out tomorrow!" Adam toasted loudly as he dropped his shot into the mug.

"Salute," they all cheered.

They clashed their mugs and followed the first drink with a second boilermaker. Khan was challenged as he did everything in his power to not throw up.

"So, Frankie tells me that you guys might need some help out here? Somewhere to crash and lay low?" Adam asked as they all sat down and made themselves comfortable.

"We were told that you're a good person to know out here," Fabian replied.

"I could be," Adam said to him, looking at his cousin with a smile.

"What does that mean?" Khan asked him.

"What it means is that you have a problem that I might be able to help you out with, and I have a problem that you guys might be able to help me out with," Adam answered.

"Well, you know what we're up against. What's your dilemma?" Sebastian asked.

As he looked around to ensure that there were no prying eyes, Adam leaned forward on the table and looked at the four who were listening attentively. "Several years ago, I got into the numbers game with this guy I met in the state pen. We did pretty good for a little while, until he decided to bring in his former cellmate to help out with the Latin market."

"Latin market? There's a Latin market out here?" Sebastian asked out of curiosity.

"There is," Adam replied with an ambiguous smile.

"So, what's the problem?" Fabian asked.

"Well, you know, white boys from the other side of town. Trying to get a piece of the action can often prove difficult. You know how you people are…"

"No, I don't—how are we?" Fabian questioned.

"You know, that fucking machismo bullshit that you guys carry around like an oxygen tank; which, by the way, you guys really need to tone that shit down a little. The whole world gets it and, quite frankly, we really don't give a shit about it. That goes for you too, Frankie. Remember, you're only half-Polish."

After several seconds of the four fiercely staring at Adam, Sebastian, who couldn't help but agree with him, said, "Go on."

"Well, here in St. Paul's, we do things a little different. We're not like Minneapolis, or a big city like Chicago that has an unlimited amount of resources to conduct business with for guys like us. Instead, we're limited down here to feel comfortable with the little we have. It removes a lot of the animosities that are associated with the business," Adam tried explaining.

"What does that have to do with the Latin community?"

"Well, with me on this side of the fence and my buddy from the pen forming commerce on the Spanish side of town, together we've done well," Adam continued as he took a hefty swig of his beer.

"Sounds good, so what's the problem?" Sebastian asked.

"The problem is that I haven't heard from my buddy for several weeks now; presumably dead for all I know. There's this guy that has pretty much taken over on that side of the operation, and word on the street is that he wants to branch out over on this side."

"So take the fucker of the equation," Frankie said to him.

"I would love to, but on that side of town they'll spot me a mile away. Not to mention, they know who I am."

"So what are you asking of us?" Sebastian probed as he leaned back in his lounge chair.

"Well, this guy, David Martinez, is one of your people."

"One of my people? What the hell does that mean?" Sebastian asked with an offended tone.

"What I mean is that it will be a lot easier for you boys to infiltrate that community, accomplish that removal and resume a business over there—which is untapped, by the way. Believe me when I tell you, they will not see you coming," Adam replied with a suggestive smile.

"I don't know," Khan said, showing signs of not wanting involvement.

"What's in it for us?" Fabian asked.

"Twenty percent."

"You think we're going to risk our asses for twenty percent?" Khan loudly interjected, causing a few people to take notice.

"Forty percent," Fabian earnestly negotiated.

"What the fuck. Hell no, twenty percent is more than generous, especially for some outsiders," Adam replied.

"Fuck that, you can do it yourself then," Sebastian fired back.

"Sebastian, we need his help. You know this," Frankie calmly explained. "I vouch for my cousin and I'm sure we can all benefit from this. So, let's just compromise, and meet in the middle. Thirty percent," he says to them all.

Like a Mexican standoff, waiting to see who pulls the trigger first, all of them remained silent in anticipation of a verbal agreement that would unite them and form an alliance. Then, a barmaid, unsuspecting of the negotiations, returned with a fresh round of drinks.

"Are you boys okay? Looks pretty intense in here, especially considering all these pretty faces around you, looking for a good time tonight," she said to them all as she placed the fresh drinks on the table and removed the empty glasses.

Without visually straying away or showing any signs of defeat, Adam raised his mug of beer in the air and declared, "Thirty percent?"

Sebastian, who glanced at his brothers and Frankie, lifted his mug in agreement. "Thirty percent."

Like fearless gladiators, ardent in their allegiance and common treaty, the newly-formed St. Paul warriors, valiant and stout, dropped their whiskey shots into their mugs. Together, they saluted their fresh alliance by guzzling snifter bombs for the rest of the night.

Chapter VIII

Reputation Is Everything

"You think he's on to us? I mean, he's always looking around," Fabian said to Sebastian as he leaned his head back, trying not to be seen.

"Fabe, he can't see us. We're parked almost two blocks away," Sebastian replied as he racked his pistol.

"You know, Fabe might be right. You never know," Khan said. He was fidgeting from side to side in the back seat, preparing himself to exit the car.

"If you think about it, he's nervous right about now. That little business of his wasn't inherited, you know," Fabian remarked.

"Well, let's be careful—this isn't Chicago," Khan said to Fabian as he continued fidgeting in the back seat.

"You know, I have an uncle that suffered the same thing that you're suffering from," Frankie said to Khan. He was also sitting in the back seat, staring at Khan's every discomforted move. "He used to walk around with baby wipes to alleviate that sort of thing."

"What sort of thing is that, Frankie?" Khan asked, annoyed.

"Whoa, don't get upset, Khan. I'm just saying that if you're experiencing discomfort or something, perhaps properly wiping might be useful for you."

Khan, who displayed an annoyed look, saw from the rearview mirror that his brother was looking at him with a smirk.

"What the fuck are you looking at, Fabian?"

"What?" Fabian responded, quickly looking away.

"For your information, we have been in this car for well over eight hours, waiting for this son of a bitch to come out. So, excuse me for being little uncomfortable," Khan loudly said to them, causing them to remain quiet for a few minutes.

"I'm just saying that you'd be surprised what a little—"

"Fuck you, you fucking kielbasa-black-bean-eating motherfucker!" Khan angrily yelled as he got out of the car.

"Khan, where are you going?" Sebastian yelled after him.

"Frankie, you're a fucking asshole!" he irately said to Frankie before they were all forced to exit the vehicle.

"Khan, Khan, take it easy," Sebastian said as he caught to his brother.

"Oh shit, Sebastian, there he is," Fabian alerted him, preparing the others to follow their intended target.

But Khan, who was heated by Frankie's infuriating banter, continued walking toward their target: David Martinez.

"Khan, slow the hell down," Fabian warned him for the sake of not being made out.

Sebastian and Frankie, who realized that calming Khan down was hopeless, quickly ran across the street to beat Khan to the punch, so that they could make it a quiet and quick kill.

David Martinez was already a paranoid individual and noticed from his peripheral vision that he was being followed by someone. Immediately stopping to remove a pack of cigarettes and light one up, he casually looked around and noticed that both Sebastian and Frankie had stopped.

"Oh, these sons of bitches think they can fuck with me?" he thought to himself as he started walking the busy streets of Minneapolis.

David Martinez also saw both Khan and Fabian closing in, and he removed a small pistol from his waist while slowly walking away from his aggressors. Then, giving up on the notion that he would get away, he lifted his gun in the air to confront Sebastian and Frankie, who were just feet away from him. "You want to fuck with me, come get some!"

With his gun now exposed, he started backing away between two parked cars, not paying attention to the oncoming traffic. Just like that, a warehouse food truck smashed his head on the windshield and splattered blood alongside parked cars.

Sebastian and Frankie, caught by the surprise of their target's careless demise, remained mesmerized. They stared at Martinez's head, split open and embedded in the windshield until the weight from his body peeled him off and lay him flat on the street.

Horrifying screams erupted from the witnessing public all around the blood-stained streets. Sebastian and Frankie looked across the street to see Khan and Fabian turn around and walk toward their car. The two friends began to panic as the spectators formed a circle around David Martinez's body and began looking at them, placing the pieces together.

"Sebastian, let's get the hell out of here."

Sebastian, who kept replaying the gory image instilled in his head in slow-motion, slowly walked away and disappeared into the heard of spectators rushing to see what appeared to be a freak and unfortunate accident.

"What the hell happened?" Fabian asked as Sebastian and Frankie entered the vehicle.

"That dumbass pulled out on us, slowly walked backward without looking behind him and, before he was able to point his gun at us, kissed the windshield, that stupid fuck," Sebastian explained.

"No, what happened was we got rid of Adam's problem and opened up a profitable opportunity for all of us," Frankie said to them with a smile.

"Well, let's head back to St. Paul's. Us being around this neighborhood is getting me nervous," Khan said to them.

25 Minutes Later

"Hey, Frankie, how you doing?" Adam nervously asked his cousin as he walked into the apartment.

"Doing pretty good. To be honest with you, I could sure use a drink. Maybe we can go to the bar and have those boiler makers we had a week ago."

"Where are the guys?"

"They'll be here shortly. Are you okay, Adam? You seem a little nervous."

"Yeah, I'm good."

"Adam, what's up?" Fabian asked him, as the three brothers walked into Adam's apartment and began removing their pistols and knives.

"What's up, fellas? I heard everything went well today," Adam said, trying not to show any signs of apprehension.

"Yeah, that's one way of putting it," Fabian replied, smiling at Sebastian and Frankie.

"Well, the word on the street is that it was pretty gory," explained Adam.

"What do you mean? What exactly did you hear, and from whom?" Khan asked.

"The word went out from his people that he was pushed in front of a delivery truck in the middle of Fourteenth Street," Adam nervously told him, studying Khan's facial expressions.

"Who the hell told you that?" Khan replied.

"Well…" Adam mumbled.

"What my brother is trying to say is that we didn't think there would be any witnesses," Sebastian intervened. He looked at Frankie, Fabian, and Khan, and smiled at Adam.

"This all took place on a busy street near where he lives, and when someone is thrown, pushed, or what have you, in front of a moving vehicle, the chances of having a witness is probable."

"Well, Adam, from what you're telling me it seems that you're not happy with the end results," Sebastian said. He sat down at the small kitchen table, crossed his legs and lit up a cigarette.

"Oh, no, I'm very happy; however, I didn't think you were going to kill him that way. I thought you would just shoot him with a silencer or something. You know, the old-fashioned way."

"Well, Adam, we had all intentions to do that; however, we felt that sending a message as stern as we did would deter anyone who is considering taking over the helm, in the event that their boss is taken out," Sebastian explained.

"Yeah, it cries out that 'this can happen to you if you fuck with us'," Fabian added.

"Well, I do believe that your point was made because his people want to work with us."

"Excellent!" Frankie said to his cousin as he patted him on the back.

"You guys are fucking sick."

"No, Adam, this is the life we've chosen, and this is the way things are done. And if you want to make it in this business, you better prepare to make tough decisions, including removing someone from the equation. Now, if you don't mind, let's go out and celebrate our new joint venture, our thirty percent and your new territory," said Sebastian with a victorious smile.

Chapter IX

A Chihuahua Against A Pit Bull

"How's the old man?" Heiman asked Avner's son, Myles, who had been near his father's bedside for several days with his mother and several other siblings.

"Last night wasn't a good night. His blood pressure was dangerously low, and his breathing is getting worse, even with that stupid respirator machine thing shoved down his throat," he replied to Heiman, who was also suffering from sleepless nights since the ordeal.

"My wife made some chicken soup and was up all night making Teiglach. Please, give this to your mother, you guys need to eat," Heiman said as he removed a pot from a brown shopping bag.

"Thanks, Heime, but right now I just don't have the appetite; especially knowing that someone out there wanted my father dead...my dad. I mean, this man is known and well-respected in the neighborhood. He's no rookie, you know."

"I know," Heiman replied to him, patting him on the shoulder for comfort. "Look, I have to continue with the business—you know what happens when the cat leaves."

"Yeah, I know. Again, thank you, and Lilah Tov."

"We're good. Lilah Tov," Heiman replied as he tapped him on the cheek and began to walk away. "Oh, Myles, one more thing: Sean McLoughlin—you know, the one that everyone calls Red—he's going to be coming by shortly and will hang around to help out."

"Heiman, he's not our people."

"Myles, let me tell you something that I think you're overlooking. Red was with your father when this all went down."

"But he's not the one that's lying in the hospital room."

"Myles, there were several people in that room that did and didn't get out alive."

"Speaking of which, anything on those momzer-spic fucks?"

"Myles, as soon as I hear something, I'll call you."

"Please do that."

"Oh, look who's here," Heiman pointed out to Myles as he watched Red walk toward them with a box of brewed coffee.

"What, you get lost?"

"Sorry, Heiman, but I forget how bad traffic is here."

"Never mind that. I have to go back to the club and handle some business. Do not leave their sight until I tell you," Heiman ordered him with a straight face.

Red, who felt for a brief moment that something wasn't right, dismissed it when he saw Myles walking back in the hospital room. "Heiman, what's wrong?"

"I'm sorry, kid. I'm just tired, cranky and old."

"Heime, go home and get some sleep."

"Once I'm done at the club I'll go home and sleep for a little while. Have you heard anything?"

"No. Total communication blackout, one hundred percent."

Heiman did not like his response and just stared at him for several seconds, looking into Red's eyes to see if he could pick up any disingenuousness.

"See you later, big boy."

"See you later, Heime."

"How's he doing?" Red asked Myles as he quietly walked into the room.

"I wish I knew," Myles replied, staring out the hospital window.

"Hey, Myles, if there's anything I can do—"

"As a matter of fact, there is, Red, Sean, whatever they call you!" he said sternly to him.

"I know you know where these buddies of yours are at, or have an idea where they could be at, and you need to tell us."

"Myles, whether want to believe this or not, your father has been good to me since I was been a young boy. Not to mention, he's been good to Sebastian, Khan, Fabian and even Frankie. We've all been with your pops since day one and have done a lot of work for him. Do you honestly believe they or I would do something like this?"

Myles went back in time to an event that took place during his bar mitzvah, involving Red and the boys. It was an event that got him into serious trouble with his dad. He paused for several seconds as he questioned their involvement with the hit placed on his father.

"Fuck!" Myles yelled out, slamming the room door open and exiting out.

Red was a little thrown off by this disingenuous reaction and paused as he watched the door slowly close.

"Sean," a weakened, raspy voice called for him, using a name not called out by many.

"Sean," it called out to him for the second time.

"My love," Avner's wife said as she and loved ones gathered around the bed.

"We thought we lost you. We love you so much," she said to her husband as she kissed and hugged him.

Avner was sincerely grateful for his family being there, but looked at Red, for he was the first thing he remembered about the ordeal.

"Where's Moshe?" Avner asked with a weak voice.

"He just stepped out," his wife replied. "Sean, will you go out and get him," she requested.

Right before Red was going to head out, Myles walked in, looked at his father and dropped to his knees, motioning in gratefulness. God had answered his prayers.

"Moshe," Avner called him, a name that had not been used since his bar mitzvah.

"Pop," he answered as he got up to hug his father. "I didn't think I—"

"It's okay. I know," Avner said to him, silencing the very idea.

"Is everyone okay?"

"Abner didn't make it," Myles said to him, saddened.

Avner sighed and leaned his head back, thinking about his old childhood friend, Abner, who had been part of the business that spanned more than four decades. He realized this was not going to end well for anyone.

"Do me a favor and get Khan; there are a couple of things I need him to do for me."

The long, disappointed look from his son, coupled with the look on Red's face, caused Avner to start remembering the shooting. He remained quiet for several seconds, fearing that Khan was among those shot dead.

"Khan is on the run," Red reluctantly told him.

"I need everyone out," Avner demanded in a weakened voice, watching his wife and most of the others surrounding him leave the room

"Raise this stupid thing up," he continued, trying to elevate the back part of the bed. "And what the hell do you mean that Khan is on the run?"

"It is believed that Sebastian, Fabian, and Frankie had something to do with what took place at your office," Red explained.

"What the hell are you talking about? They would never do that."

"I don't know, dad. All we know is what Heiman is telling us."

"Does he have proof? Did he see them pull the trigger?" Avner asked, unconvinced.

"I don't know, Avvi," Red said to Avner, but staring directly at Myles.

"What the hell are you talking about, Red? You all grew up together. You guys even joined the military together. Not to mention, Fabian is your best friend. Do you really believe that these guys would do that?" Avner asked him, not wanting to believe what he considered unwarranted news.

"Avvi, you already know the answer to that, but Heiman is hell-bent and is using a lot of resources to have them killed. There's nothing I can do about it," replied Red with a frustrated look.

A knock on the door ceased their conversation.

"I know you hebs don't believe that the real messiah already came to the world, but perhaps some consideration might be in order," Antonio Mancini announced as he slowly walked in to visit his longtime associate.

"Hey, Tony, how you doing?" Myles greeted him.

"So, how's the old man?"

"The old man is okay for now and will make it, but I'm so sorry about your nephew," Avner replied as he extended shaking hands to greet Antonio.

"Avvi, it's good to see you all right, my old friend. And thank you. However, this loss is not one I accept. It was brutal and uncalled for," Antonio Mancini said to Avner as he pulled up a seat near the hospital bed.

"You remember Red, right?" Avner asked him as he realized Red was not greeted.

"How can I not remember the big guy? How you doing?" he reluctantly replied.

Antonio gave a silent stare that placed everyone in an uncompromising situation. Without concern for anything or anyone around him, only to the situation that involved his beloved nephew, he sighed deeply. "What the fuck happened? Tell me that you had nothing to do with this, Avvi?"

"Tony, I'm not going to lie. It was brought to my attention; not about your nephew, but about some Greek guy," Avner immediately told him.

"Yeah, his name was Stelios," Antonio replied with an impassive look.

"This is what I'm talking about, I don't know what went down with that," Avner said.

"Yeah, it was about him," Antonio began explaining. "He owed me a lot of cash for a long time, and I didn't want to hurt my nephew's feelings, so I spoke to your people who agreed to help out. On that very day, I carefully explained

Stelios' whereabouts. I even mentioned the time and the clothing description."

"I need more time, Tony. I'm sure we can resolve this," Avner pleaded with him, realizing that, in the end, everything was linked to him.

"Avvi, our families have been working with each other for a real long time and I'm sure we will address this one way or another. With that being said, once the identity is revealed, you need to bring him to me. No exceptions!"

Without saying a word, Avner, physically weakened by his ordeal, nodded his head in approval.

"Well, if you don't mind, I have a funeral to attend to. So, Avvi. I am happy that you are well, and I am confident this will be handled appropriately. Please give my best to the Mrs." Antonio said as he placed his chair back and began to walk out of the room without looking at anyone.

"One last thing," Antonio said, directing his attention to Red before leaving to meet up with his bodyguards waiting outside the door. "I know that those reckless-ass clowns are your friends and you all have been there for each other for some time. But tell me, do you believe that they are incapable of following simple instructions? Or was any of this done intentionally?"

"I've known them for a—"

"Whoa, whoa, whoa, it's a yes or no question," Antonio interrupted him.

"No."

"I don't care what has to be done, but this needs to get fixed, and get fixed real quick, before a war between two families that have been at peace for decades begins. Do you understand me?" And with that, Antonio Mancini was gone.

"Pop, what are we going to do?" Myles asked.

"It's not what we're going to do, it's what needs to be done," Avner replied as he looked at Red.

"Well, I think it's all bullshit anyway," Myles said. "I mean, who gives a fuck about these Guinea fucks anyway? It's not like they have muscle the way they used to back in the day. The Russians or the slops, yeah, I understand, but them?"

"Listen to me, you little fucking shlemiel. I love you and I know you mean well, but you are a Chihuahua against a pit bull, do you understand me?" Avner asked his son with a wheezing cough.

"You're getting too involved, and these people will annihilate you. This is the very reason why I never wanted this for you—it's the very reason why I'm putting you through law school."

"Pop, why do you disrespect me like that?"

"You're not listening to me. It's not that you are not capable, I know you are, but this is different. It's become personal."

"So, how do you expect me to figure all this out? Let alone find Khan and the rest of his brothers?"

"With his help," Avner replied to his son, looking at Red.

Red, who did not like where the conversation was heading, stared at Avner with a disappointed look.

"Sean, listen to me because I'm on borrowed time. You and the rest of the boys have been very loyal to me;

however, I need for you to find them. If they are responsible, you know what needs to be done, no matter how much it might hurt you," he said to Red, knowing his young accomplice wanted no part of it.

"But if they aren't, what's gonna happen? Are you going to clear their names?"

"I really don't know if there will be any name-clearing on this one," Avner explained to him, knowing it was not the answer Red wanted to hear. "When this is all over, I'm going to release you and give you my blessing to start your own crew. That's what all of you have been wanting, right?"

"Avvi, we're happy with the way things are," Red replied.

"Oh, stop with that bullshit. I was young once and wanted the same thing," Avner said to him with an emotional stare. "There are many things that I have done in my life that are questionable, and soon enough, like all men, I will have to answer to God. But, my time on earth is soon coming to an end, and I have to let it all go."

Avner began to cough with great difficulty, but continued talking to Red.

"I love all of you, whether you wish to believe it or not. But leaving what took me years to build to these pasta slurping dagos, so they can take over and dismantle it, is something that will not happen. So keep in mind: it's either you correct this, or you go down as a culprit. All eyes are on you. You know what you have to do, and what needs to be done. Your existence relies on it."

"Thank you, Avvi."

"Don't thank me yet, because this isn't over. Keep in mind, there will be a successor to this family, and I can assure you both families will need to unite peacefully. Now go, I am very tired and need to rest," Avner said to Red as he lowered his bed. He turned to his son and requested,

"Moshe, go get your mother."

"Pop, what about Heime?"

"There's no stopping him now. I'll have to deal with him on another level."

Chapter X

Brooklyn Park

"Frankie, I know in Chicago winters can be brutal, but this shit up here is fucking ridiculous. I mean, look at this. We came here around, what, early October? And we're now in March, and there is absolutely no sign of thawing out. I mean, what the hell? I'm losing my mind up here with all this freaking snow," Sebastian complained as he sipped his coffee and looked out the window.

"It's the way things are up here, Sebastian. You get used to it."

"No, Frankie, this is crazy. I mean, one week it's an Alberta Clipper, and the week after that, it's a freaking Panhandle Hook. What the hell is that shit all about? It doesn't fucking end."

"Well, we're in March now and pretty soon we'll see warmer days."

"Warmer days, my ass!" Sebastian shouted out in frustration.

"Well, at least some people around here enjoy it more than others," Frankie commented, referring to Fabian as he looked over the local paper.

"That's another thing that's driving me crazy out here, Frankie. Humping on big women like that is not normal. What the hell is wrong with that kid?"

"You know your brother, he loves that rhino-riding bullshit. It's who he is."

"Frankie, wake him up."

"Screw you, you wake him up. He's your brother."

"I did it the last two days, and I swear to you, man: I cannot get that mental image out of my head. Please, Frankie, get him up. You know he doesn't have a clock in his room, and we have to go to the bar soon for our daily collections."

"You know, if it weren't for me visually seeing those women, I would have thought that your brother was into men because it smells like pure ass in there," said Frankie as he took a big swig of his coffee.

"Are you going to wake him up or not?" Sebastian sternly asked.

"Fine, but just know that I will have met my weekly wake-up quota. Get Khan or my cousin to do it for the rest of the week, because after this, I'm done," Frankie irritably replied, mentally preparing himself for his entry to Fabian's room.

"Fabe, you up?" he called out as he softly knocked on the door.

"Fabe, it's time to get up," Frankie called for the second time as he peeked his head inside the bedroom door and saw Fabian lying on the bed.

Sebastian, who wanted to see no part of the disturbing visual, motioned Frankie to push open the door wider so as to let some of the foul order out.

"You owe me!" Frankie whispered to Sebastian. "Fabe, you up?" he called again as he inspected the inside of the bedroom.

"Damn," Frankie mumbled to himself. He looked at Fabian sleeping in the nude with two large-sized women sleeping naked next to him on a queen-size bed that showed weight fatigue.

"What the hell are you looking at?" one of the women said to Frankie when she saw him staring at them in the mirror. "What, you want some?" she insolently asked.

"Sweetheart, he can't handle any of this," Fabian said to her, slapping her on the ass.

Frankie displayed facial signs of disgust as he inspected the large-sized ladies' thong underwear and bras thrown on the floor from the drunken night before.

"Fabe, it smells like ass in here."

"How would you know? When was the last time you even had some ass?" one of the women said, and they all giggled at his expense.

"Hey, man, it's about time to go and collect. Besides, it's your turn to shovel the front of the building and at the bar."

"Frankie, do me a big solid and do it for me? I'll do it when your turn comes up."

"No-can-do, Fabe. I'll be busy in the bathroom rinsing my eyes out with bleach."

"Come on, Frank, can't you see I'm busy?"

"Busy doing what? Planning out their feeding times? No way!"

"Fuck you, asshole!" one of Fabian's women shouted.

"No, Fabian has that all worked out for you ladies."

"Fine, give me a minute while I hump one out."

"Shit, Fabe, is that what you call it?" Frankie sarcastically said to Fabian as he walked out and slammed the door.

"We need to have an intervention with your brother," Frankie said to Sebastian, who was standing on the opposite side of the living room, appalled.

Sebastian was about to answer him but became distracted by the sexual moaning of one of the women being sexually pleasured while the other coached on in encouragement.

"Hey guys, I got some fresh bread for breakfast," Khan happily said to them as he walked into the apartment with Adam.

The four, who knew that Fabian was doing his dirty deeds, all stared at the closed bedroom door in horror.

"Is that the two...whatever you want to call them, from last night?" Khan reluctantly asked.

"I don't know about last night, but what's happening in there is not right," Frankie replied.

Then, like a whale blowing out its blowhole while surfacing for the ocean deep, one of the women screamed out in contentment.

"Okay, okay, it's my turn!" the other woman eagerly screamed out.

"Come on and let's hurry up," Fabian said to her in a fatigued voice, indicating he was short on time and tired.

"Look, I don't know about you guys, but I no longer have an appetite and will shovel the front," Frankie said to them all as he began to put his jacket on.

"I'll join you," Adam said.

"Khan and I will do the bar front," Sebastian remarked as they all walked out the front door.

Two Hours Later

"What the hell do you mean he hasn't paid us?" Sebastian questioned Khan, annoyed about a customer who was two days late in paying a gambling debt.

"Like I said: the son of a bitch hasn't paid us in two days, and he's one of Fabian's people."

"Who is one of my people?" Fabian asked as he walked into the bar.

"Well look who's here—it's the zaftig whisperer," Frankie commented with a laugh as he counted money.

Fabian, who smiled at the very idea that loving plus size woman was something that was an acquired taste, ignored his best friend and addressed his brother Khan. "So, who is one of my people? Did somebody not pay up?"

"As a matter of fact, he is one of your people. You know that guy Rick that is always sweating when he eats and gawks at the barmaids? He's two days behind on payment for the Wild's loss."

"He'll pay up," Fabian confidently replied.

"Yes, he will, Fabe. As soon as you go over there and get our money," Sebastian replied in a demanding tone.

"Jeez, why don't we just wait for him here? Sooner or later he'll show up."

"Because he hasn't been here in two days; not to mention that he owes us five large," Sebastian explained to him with an annoyed look.

"Fine, I'll go and get the money."

"I'll go with you," Adam said as he put his coat on. "That fat fuck isn't taking our operation serious, so I'll remind him that money is always due the day of or the day after placing bets."

"How far is he?" Khan asked.

"Brooklyn Park."

"Where the hell is that?" Sebastian asked. The name grabbed his attention.

"It's out in the burbs, not far from here," Adam replied as he pulled his pistol slide back to confirm there was a cartridge in the chamber.

"Alright, just watch each other's backs out there. When it comes to large sums of money like this, having someone pay for it is never a smooth transition, which is the reason why that fat fuck hasn't shown his face around here," Sebastian explained to them.

"Well, since you know where this Brooklyn Park is at, you can drive," said Fabian as he walked out the door.

* *

"So, how do you want to handle this?" Adam asked Fabian with a stressed look.

"Are you okay, Adam? You seem a little nervous."

"Well, excuse me for not being used to this kind of shit. You do know that before you guys came here, this type of business interaction did not happen," he replied as he looked around their surroundings.

"Look, we're going to go in, in a non-threatening manner. Once we see him, we'll ask if he's okay, and sternly ask for our money."

"What if he doesn't have our money?"

"Based on how he comes to the bar and splurges on food and drink, and now seeing how he lives in this nicely maintained neighborhood, I have a feeling that he'll be able to pay us."

"You have a point, Fabian."

"Alright, let gets our mind in the game, get our money and get out of here. I'm starting to shake from not eating," Fabian said as he adjusted himself and knocked on the door.

"Maybe he's sleeping?" Adam remarked. They heard the television playing inside in the background, but nobody answered after several knocks.

Fabian looked around and made sure that there wasn't anyone looking, before taking out his wallet and removing a pick blade to unlock the door.

Adam, who just decided to see if the door was open, turned the door handle and found that it was unlocked. He smiled at Fabian.

"Hey, Rick, you home?" Adam called out.

"Hello, is anyone home?" Fabian asked aloud as he looked inside the kitchen that showed no sign of usage.

Then, realizing that the television they heard was coming from the bedroom, Adam motioned at Fabian and pointed at the bedroom door.

"Yo, Rick, are you alright?" Adam shouted out as he slowly pushed the door open.

"Shit!" Adam loudly whispered, startled by the scene in front of him. An extremely large man was lying on the bed, facedown, with what appeared to be a thin, young girl's hand sticking out from underneath his midsection.

Fabian and Adam immediately drew their weapons and tactfully cleared the small two bedroom apartment, looking for any hostiles hiding inside.

"We're clear, Fabe," Adam said, putting his pistol away. "This is not good!"

"Come help me move this fat fuck off the bed," Fabian directed as they both rushed back into the bedroom.

After forcefully prying the man's dead body off the bed and landing him on the floor, Adam placed his hands over his head in panic. "What the fuck did we just walk into?"

"I don't know but this fat fuck is a Chester!" Fabian said to Adam, placing his hands on the young girl's neck to feel for a pulse.

"Fabian, this is not good. This is a motherfucking crime scene."

"Look, there's a purse on the nightstand. Open it and see if there's an I.D. or something," he asked Adam. "No, no, no, not with your hands. Use that fat fuck's smelly shirt to open it."

Adam, who began to uncontrollably shake, managed to open the purse after several attempts and looked at the girl's driver's license.

"Fuck, this girl just barely turned seventeen?" Adam whispered out.

"Adam, we have to get the hell out of here!"

"Yeah, I agree, let's go!"

"Wait, let's see if there's any money or something. I mean, we're already here, we might as well see if we can retrieve our money."

"Are you fucking kidding me?" Adam asked, giving Fabian a shocked and appalled look.

"No, I'm not. Let's just quickly look around and then we'll leave. It's not like people know that we're here."

"Fine, but let's make it quick," Adam replied, still reluctant.

After several minutes of carefully searching the bedroom, Fabian found an envelope inside a jacket, hung inside the closet door. Written on it were the words: "Rod. Brothers."

"You see, he had all intentions of paying us back," Fabian said with a smile.

"Good, Fabian. I'm so happy for you," Adam sarcastically replied.

"You know, Adam, she kind of has a nice rack on her."

"Dude, you have some serious fucking issues, man!"

"I'm just saying. I mean, look at him. How on earth would a hairy back, fat fucking polar bear like him ever have had the chance to score like this?" Fabian asked.

"The only way he could have accomplished such a thing is to pay for services that we provided," an Eastern European voice replied.

"Oh, shit," both Fabian and Adam uttered as they both drew their guns and pointed at two men who had quietly entered the bedroom.

"Who the fuck are you?" Adam asked, walking away from the window to remove himself as a target.

"Please, gentlemen, I did not come here to be confrontational or become a threat. I come here to get Alica," the same man replied to Adam with an insincere smile.

"Who the hell is Alica?" Fabian asked, never losing his front sight on his target.

"She is the dead girl on the bed. She belongs to me; or at least, she used to belong to me."

"You're her pimp?" Adam asked.

"Pimp is such a derogatory word. It's a word Americans use."

"Then what do you call it?"

"I see it as more like what you Americans call a chaperone."

"Chaperone? Whatever. How can we help you, Mr. Chaperone?" Adam asked.

"Well, I originally came for the girl to make sure she was okay, but I can see that she has had some better days, yes?"

"We had nothing to do with this, I can assure you. We just came for some money this fat fuck owed us," Fabian explained, hoping he could calm the intensity between him, Adam and the bellicose-looking bodyguard that accompanied the shorter chieftain man who was doing the talking.

"So, you say that he owed you money, yes?"

"That doesn't concern you," Fabian immediately fired back.

"In my country, to disrespect a man in such a manner comes with severe consequences. Do you understand my friend?" he asked Fabian.

"Well, then we might have a problem," Adam replied.

"Whoa, whoa, whoa, don't move, big boy," Fabian shouted out as he watched the bodyguard motioning to slip his hand into his coat pocket.

"Snadný. Když vám řeknu, ujistěte se, že oba střílet do hlavy." (Easy. When I tell you, make sure you shoot them both in the head.)

"What the fuck did you just say?" Fabian nervously asked.

"I was just telling my comrade that we do not have to worry about you two. You have nothing to do with any of this," he explained to Fabian, hoping he could get him to calm down.

"Listen here, Nikolai, do me a favor and don't insult my intelligence. If it were the other way around, I would start telling myself, 'dead men tell no tales'!"

"Where I am from, we do things a little differently my friend," he started to say to Fabian, but stopped mid-sentence at the sound of Rick waking up and moaning from a conscious state.

"Son of a bitch," Fabian mumbled, looking down at the stirring Rick.

"Nyn!" (Now!) came the order for the bodyguard to shoot Fabian, who was distracted by Rick waking up from the dead.

Then, like a sawed timber falling straight to the ground, the massive bodyguard plummeted to his demise as a result of a gunshot to the head. Fabian defensively backed away and raised his pistol, ready to shoot the remaining Eastern European threat.

"What the fuck?" Fabian shouted at Adam.

"You forget that I'm Polish, and I was able to pick up on a lot of what this fuck was saying. Believe me when I tell you, they were going to take us out, so I took him out first," explained Adam to Fabian, who was startled.

"Jesteś tak godny jak pies." (You are as worthy as a dog.)

"Ahh, you speak Polish as well?" Adam said to the man ordering to shoot.

"Only when I fuck Polish whores!" he replied, a vengeful look in his eyes.

"What the fuck are they?" Fabian tensely asked.

"They're from the Czech Republic," Adam answered.

"I cannot place it together, but I know you. And when I figure it out, I can assure you that you will suffer greatly!" the Eastern European threat said to Fabian as he studied Fabian, trying to recognize him.

"Well, I guess we'll never know, will we?" Fabian said as he pointed his gun, ready to shoot.

"If I were you, I would seriously consider who it is you are pointing that gun at."

"Fabian, don't do it," Rick whispered as he slowly tried to regain his balance.

"You stupid motherfucker! You're going to call me out by name?" Fabian angrily yelled at Rick. "You know what, we already have what we came for, and your existence in this world is pointless!"

"No, Fabian, no, no, no!" Rick screamed out as he realized that Fabian was going to shoot him.

Just as Fabian was about to pull the trigger, he felt a bullet zip alongside his arm, striking Rick in the eye socket. The blood splatter was rapid, foul and unanticipated. It splashed on the wall, causing Fabian to become nauseated and frightened by the brain matter and bone fragmentation.

"Shit, Fabe, let's get the fuck out of here," Adam yelled. He grabbed Fabian and pulled him away from the window, avoiding several sniper shots breaching the bedroom window, with them as the intended target.

Fabian lifted his pistol to shoot at his Czech Republic target but was shot in the chest, causing him to crash on the glass living room table.

Adam, who witnessed the Czech gangster shoot Fabian and run out of the apartment, ran to Fabian's aid.

"Fabian!" Adam yelled out in panic.

"I'm okay, he got me in the vest. Shit, this hurts," Fabian yelled out, feeling the bullet lodged in his vest. "Help me the fuck up and let's get the hell out of here."

"What the fuck are we going to do?" Adam asked. Looking around the apartment, he realized that there were very few options of escape.

"Let's go up to the roof and cross over all the way to the end. We'll exit out that way," Fabian suggested.

"Are you serious?"

Fabian, who could only smile as he was reminded of what took place not long ago, rubbed his chest in pain. "Trust me, it'll work...I hope," he said to Adam as he carefully looked out the door, before running up the stairs, toward the roof.

"Shh," Fabian whispered when they reached the rooftop. He placed his finger over his lips before mumbling, when they reached the rooftop.

"Shit." There was an alarm system on the rooftop door.

"What the hell are we going to do?" Adam asked, looking between the steps to see if anyone was coming up the stairs.

Fabian, who was listening closely to the outside environment, decided to take a chance and open the door, hoping the alarm wouldn't sound off.

"Fabian, I see a set of hands slowly making their way up the stairs. Whatever it is we're going to do, we need to do it now."

"Well, I'm not going out like that, so here goes nothing," Fabian replied as he slowly pushed the door open. His chance paid off.

"Adam, c'mon, let's go," Fabian whispered, grabbing his accomplice by the shirt collar.

"Fabian, I hope this works, because I haven't run in years and I'm already tired."

Fabian looked at how far the distance was to the other end of the rooftop and realized that nothing could be used to conceal their movements. He became immediately discouraged at the probability of them being shot at in the open.

"You better get your oversized body across this roof or deal with the consequences."

"Fabian, I'm not joking, I am really worn out. Damn, I never realized how out of shape I've become," Adam replied, struggling to breathe.

"Well, we can discuss that later over beer and wings, but right now we need to get out of here," Fabian said as the blaring of sirens grabbed his attention.

Adam bent over with his hands on his knees and began panting. He psychologically emboldened himself before standing erect and preparing for an imperative dash.

"Let's go," Adam said as he took a deep breath of the cold air.

Like escaped convicts, desperately running across marshlands with shackles joining them by the ankles, Fabian and Adam took off across the rooftop. Visually pathetic in their attempt to escape the clutches of their enemy, they managed to reach their destination and were content when they saw the rooftop door at the end of the adjoining building was open.

Adam, who was the first to enter the small stairway platform leading to their escape, paused to gain his mobility and waited for the spots swarming his vision to subside.

"Those damn pebbles and the ice on the rooftop kicked my ass, Fabian. I really came close to keeling over, man."

"Well, don't get too excited yet. We're not in the clear," Fabian said to him, looking between the staircase steps to see if they were clear to walk down.

"Adam…Adam!" Fabian yelled, to snap Adam back into escape mode. "I need for you to listen to me very carefully because I did not come all the way out here to get clipped by some foreigner or arrested. Do you understand me?"

"Yes," Adam replied, large beads of sweat dripping down his face.

"How is it humanly possible that you're sweating?" Fabian asked him as he stared, mesmerized. He decided to ignore it and continued with his instructions.

"Look, we're going to calmly walk down the stairs, exit out as if nothing happened and head in the opposite direction."

"What about the car? It's not like we can walk back home."

"Well, we're going to have to take a detour and go for a stroll around the neighborhood, aren't we?"

"Are you serious? It's freaking cold outside and all we have is these thin jackets because we left our coats in the car."

"What the hell are you talking about, being cold? You're sweating profusely!"

"Well, I've had a gland issue since I was a kid, and—"

"Adam, I'm not going to stand here and talk about your fucking childhood medical condition. Let's just get the hell out of here, hopefully undetected."

"Look, man, I'm sorry. I just can't get that image of that fat son of a bitch's head splattering all over the wall."

"What the hell are you talking about? You shot that guy in the head," Fabian countered as they began walking down the stairs.

"Not him, that shot was reactionary. I'm talking about Rick," Adam explained.

"Oh, yeah, I can see how the two are totally different," Fabian sarcastically replied.

"Alright, here we are. Now, remember: calmly walk out the building and start walking the opposite direction. Don't look in the direction where the car is parked, don't even fart in that direction. Just walk out acting like you live in this building, and you're going out for a walk."

"Got it," Adam confirmed.

"To je jim," (That's them) the Czech crime boss told the driver. The driver and boss were waiting on the opposite side of the street for Fabian and Adam to walk out from the building they were originally in."

"Clever opičky." (Clever little monkeys.)

"Boss, I think the big one is the numbers guy from that bar in St. Paul, near that arena on 7th Avenue."

"Are you sure?"

"I'm certain."

"You're right, because that fat prase (pig) is always in that area," the crime boss remarked.

"Do you want me to follow?"

"No. We'll meet up with them soon enough."

"What about Andrej? Are we going to leave him there and let the police investigate?"

"We have no other choice. I have to make some phone calls to clean this up, but first I have to call Andrej's brother and let him know that Andrej was killed."

The driver, who was looking in the rearview mirror at his boss speaking on the phone, glanced over the passenger side and became infuriated at the absence of his crime partner sitting there.

"Pojď me. neexistuje nic jiného, co lze udělat dnes." (Let's go. There is nothing else that can be done today.)

Chapter XI

Czech'd

"So let me get this straight—you have a dead fat fuck, and a dead Russian, or Czech or whatever-the-hell Slav country they're from?" Sebastian questioned Fabian and Adam as he tried to understand the gravity of their potentially hostile situation.

"It's not like we knew they were coming for the girl or anything. As we planned earlier, we just went to collect our money," Fabian explained as he took a swig of Jim Beam.

"Adam, you need to think and think hard about who these fuckers are. Do we need to prepare for war? Lay low?" Sebastian asked, distressed.

"Shit, I don't know. I mean, they could be from Minneapolis, Rochester, Bloomington...fuck, I don't know," Adam nervously replied, the very idea of dealing with an unknown syndicate beginning to trouble him.

"Well, were you able to at least get the money that fat pedophile fuck owed us?" Sebastian asked as he got up and joined Fabian for a drink.

"Yeah, it's right here," Fabian replied, tossing an envelope on top of the counter.

"Fuck, first Chicago and now this shit," said Sebastian, shaking his head in disbelief.

"It's probably nothing," replied Fabian as he poured another drink.

"Let me tell you something: when you come from a war-ridden country and perdition is a way of life, small-time criminals like us are expendable, do you understand me? These people are heartless," Sebastian told Fabian with a penetrating look.

"Well, you guys are well-connected, right?" Adam asked.

"Adam, let me explain something to you. We came here because of some misunderstanding; isn't that right, Fabian?" Sebastian yelled out to his little brother, never losing eye contact with Adam. "And until that misunderstanding is rectified, we are on the run, and on our own."

"So, what do we do now?" Adam asked, realizing the situation wasn't just bad—it was really fucking bad.

"We've formed a good crew out here; however, the less they know about our operation, the better off all of us are. So let's conduct business as usual, and keep our eyes and ears open," Sebastian unconvincingly explained.

"Guys, we need to talk," Khan said to them all as he walked in with a surprised look on his face.

"What's up?" Fabian asked, hoping to lighten their conversation.

"Well, I just got word that Avvi is alive."

"Are you fucking kidding me? Why are you poking your nose into something that could potentially expose us?" Sebastian asked, disappointed in his brother's carelessness.

"Well, before you jump down my throat, I was in the kitchen thinking about Janice—you know, the hospital administrator that I was banging for a little while."

"By the way, there is no proof that you even came close to hitting that sweet piece of ass," Fabian challenged him.

"You know, Fabe's right," Sebastian added.

"Fuck the two of you," Khan said with an annoyed look. "Anyhow, she doesn't know who I am outside of the book club—"

"Wait a minute, wait a minute, you belong to a book club? Are you fucking serious?"

"Sebastian, do you know about any of this?" Fabian asked.

"Are you fucking serious? You didn't know that—"

"Will the two of you shut the fuck up and let me talk?" Khan shouted in annoyance.

"Like I was saying, Janice is an administrator at that Saints Mary and Elizabeth Medical Center, and I called her because she could be trusted."

"How the hell do you know this?" Sebastian asked.

"Because she's totally in love with me and would never jeopardize what we have. I mean, she started bawling when I called her. She thought that I wanted no part of her."

"So what did she say?" Sebastian asked as he poured another drink.

"Well, I told her that I was watching the news about some old-time Mafia guy named Levine being at her hospital, and she told me they released him months ago. Then I immediately changed the conversation and started talking about her and me."

"What about you and her?" Sebastian asked.

"Well, she wants to see me, but I told her that I have a sick family member out in Colorado. She's cool, don't worry."

"The old man made it, huh? So, what now?" Sebastian asked as a hint of optimism surfaced in his demeanor, replacing the worried look he had moments ago.

"Now, I think we need to somehow find out more about what they're planning on doing."

"Khan, I know what you're thinking. You, my friend, have placed yourself on a very high pedestal, but you know damn well, as much as I do, that they are not interested in sitting all of us down to resolve any issues or misunderstanding,"

Fabian explained to his brother, hoping to bring him back down to reality.

"Maybe not them, but Red will listen."

"I don't know, Khan. Red is in a tough spot right about now, and knowing what he's going to do—or is forced to do, for that matter—is hard to call," Fabian reminded him.

"Well, we can't keep running."

"We're not. We're here in St. Paul fucking Minnesota, freezing our asses off," Sebastian said, taking another swig of his drink.

"By the way, where the hell is Frankie? I have to speak to all of you about a situation that's come up," Sebastian continued as he looked at both Fabian and Adam.

"I believe he's upstairs trying to bang that black barmaid, the one with the ass you can bounce a wrench off of," Khan informed him as he walked toward the bar for a drink.

"Listen, when Frankie is done with his jungle fever excursion, let's all meet up so that we can have our sit down to discuss concerns and planning. Something tells me that our winter thaw will reveal shit that's been covered up for some time."

Chapter XII

Mouth Full Of Metal

"Do I look like I give a fuck about your lack of knowing were Omar is?" Red asked Omar's bodyguard, who was in tears from Red grabbing his fingers. They were still healing from Frankie shooting him

"I'm telling you the truth! Omar never tells me anything, mainly because of shit like this."

"Let me explain something to you, whatever your fucking name is. You know, now that I think about it, here I am with my .45 practically shoved down your throat and I don't even know your name," Red said, mostly to himself, as he slightly pulled the pistol away from the bodyguard's face.

"So, tell me, big boy: what is your name?"

"Jashion."

"Jay-what? What the fuck are you saying? Did you just curse at me?" Red angrily asked him.

"Hey, Red, I'm just throwing it out there, but perhaps you removing the barrel of your gun out of his mouth so that he can talk a little more clearly would help? I'm just saying," Allen Morrison suggested. He was a longtime associate to Avner's operations, and had been hired to assist Red.

"You want to handle this yourself, Al? I mean, you seem to have all the fucking patience for this sort of nonsense," Red replied, frustrated.

"Whoa, whoa, whoa, don't lose a grip. I'm just saying that when there's a metal object shoved in your mouth and someone is asking you a question, responding might be a problem. That's all," he replied to Red with a smirk on his face.

Red, who didn't want to think they had been tracking Omar down all day only to come up emptyhanded, backed away to allow the bodyguard to speak. "So, what's your name, big boy?"

"Jason."

"See, that wasn't so bad, was it?" Allen asked Red.

"You know, Al, I'm getting a little fed up with your sarcastic little comments. What, like I'm stupid or something, and would have never figured out that he was unable to talk because his mouth was full of metal?"

"No, that's not what I am saying. What I'm saying is, that sometimes—"

"I really don't give a shit what you were trying to say, Al!" Red shouted as he placed the barrel of his gun back in Jason's mouth.

"So—now that I know your name, Jason—do you want to tell me where your douchebag boss can be found? I just have a couple of question to ask him," Red asked Jason.

Red tried to figure out the mumbles coming from Jason's full mouth. He knew that Allen was watching him and shaking his head in disapproval, but Red refused to turn in his direction. Eventually, Red slowly removed the pistol to allow Jason to speak.

"Shh, easy. What you say now is extremely important, because it could mean the difference between cooperation and an act of aggression. Do I make myself clear, Jason?"

Jason had been on his knees with Red holding his injured hand for well over thirty minutes as he was coldheartedly was beaten for information. However, he remained steadfast, showing that he can take a licking from the best of them.

"Jason, I don't particularly like doing this shit, especially to a big fellow like you; but make no mistake, I couldn't give a rat's ass about you, or any of Omar's people," Red explained, squatting down to Jason's eye level, showing signs of frustration.

"Now do I make myself clear?"

"Yes."

"Good, because this could have gotten really ugly," Red said as he helped Jason up to his feet, removing his vicelike grip, and sitting him down.

"Now, I hope you aren't wasting my time, because something tells me I will be out searching for my people, perhaps all night."

"Omar doesn't like including me in a lot of things. As a matter of fact, he doesn't like to include anyone," Jason explained, hoping it would not anger Red, who was still flaunting his gun.

"I understand. Go on."

"Well, the only thing I know is that he has a cousin, or someone like that, that lives in Iowa. Clinton County, if I remember correctly."

"What do you mean, 'you think'? I didn't spare your miserable life because you're not sure. I spared it because you agreed that you would be cooperative. Now, I'll ask you one last time, because I'm running out of patience: Where can my people be found?"

"Clinton County, Iowa, at his cousin's place."

"Okay, very good. Aside from your balls shrinking from the steroids you've abused throughout the years, you can rest easy knowing that your memory didn't suffer the same fate," Red said to him with a cynical look.

"Now, the only thing I need from you is the address of this cousin of Omar's that lives in Iowa," Red asked, looking at his watch and beginning to mentally prepare for what he believed was going to be a long and exhausting trip.

After a moment of silence, Red continued, "Well, unless you believe I know where this cousin of his lives at, get the fuck up, and find out the address!" He motioned for Jason to get up and look through Omar's desk drawer.

"Al, that girlfriend of yours, her cooking fucked up my stomach and now I have to take a wicked shit. What the fuck?" Red said to Allen as he closely observed Jason looking through Omar's Rolodex. Jason pulled out a business card with what he believed was the same information Omar gave Sebastian.

"You did good, Jason," Allen said, placing his pistol on the backside of his waistline, and watching Red hurry to the bathroom with great urgency.

"Now that I think about it, my girlfriend's cooking fucked my stomach up as well," Allen said to himself. He sat down on Omar's office chair, only to look up at the barrel of a gun pointed at him.

Allen, who did not show any fear, got up from his seat and began to remove his pistol from his waistline.

"Back the fuck up or I will blow your fucking head off, you cocksucker," Jason uttered out as he trembled in fear.

"You know, Jason, Red gave you the opportunity of a lifetime, and here you are fucking it all up. Now I have to get rid of you, you stupid sack of shit!"

"Fuck you, asshole!" Jason frantically yelled out as he took one step back and prepared to shoot. "It's you I'm going to get rid of."

"You're a fucking idiot," Allen said to him, annoyed. He placed his finger on the tip of the .357 revolver.

Click, click, click...

"You stupid son of a bitch! The next time you attempt to shoot someone, make sure there are bullets in your gun. Oh, never mind, there won't be a next time," Allen said before shooting him in the abdomen. The loud bang had been reduced in the fortified office.

Jason fell backward and screamed with shock as he landed in the desk chair. He examined his bloodstained hands and watched in horror as Allen fastened a silencer on his pistol.

"Fuck you, you mother—" Jason yelled out, before being silenced with a bullet to the head.

"What the fuck, Al? I go to take a shit and you kill the fucking guy. I was planning on bringing him along with us."

"Red, this guy had an extremely large gun pointed at my head. What did you expect me to do?"

"How the hell did he get a gun?" Red shakenly yelled out.

"When he went to get the business card with the address to this place we're supposed to go to written on it, he must have seen it in Omar's desk and waited for you to go to the bathroom."

As the two walked up to Omar's desk and started searching around, Allen opened up a drawer where a second gun was stored, fully loaded.

"What are the fucking chances, huh?" Allen said with a humorous grin. "I mean, look at the size of the fucking thing. That's a Smith & Wesson Model 686. That's a badass pistol, my friend."

"Look, I have to go back to the bathroom and wipe my ass. I heard a gun go off and got up mid-shit, hoping I didn't have to come out blasting," Red explained.

"I was wondering why you had one hand holding your pants and the other holding your gun," Allen said to Red as he continued searching through Omar's desk.

"Never mind wiping, I have to finish the shit first; gotta shit out all this anxiety now," Red added, nervously staring at Allen.

"Well, don't look at me. I'm not going to help you wipe your ass," Allen replied and continued searching around.

Chapter XIII

What A Way To Go

"Are you sure we're at the right place?" Red questioned Allen, as they arrived at a partially burned-out garage.

"I put the right address into the nav," Allen responded, making a U-turn to take a second look at the charred remains of what was once a garage.

"Are you sure this is the address?"

"I'm not sure now. Wait a minute and let me call Jason...oh wait, the son of a bitch is dead," Allen sarcastically replied. "This is the address on the card. Obviously there was a fire not long ago, maybe four or five months ago."

But Red, who had been an Explosive Ordnance Disposal Specialist in the Army like Khan (though they served in separate post locations), knew that this was no fire.

"Something's not right here. I mean, where are the people around this town?"

"Red, are you fucking kidding me? We're in the middle of nowhere, in West Bumfuck, Iowa, in the winter—which, by the way, is much colder than Chicago—and you're wondering where the locals are at?"

"I won't argue with you, it's very cold here," Red said to him, continuing to look around.

"No, Red, it's colder than a witch's tit out here; I mean, I have the heater on and I can still see my breath inside the car."

"Shit, this sucks," Red mumbled. The very idea of running into a roadblock did not settle well with him.

"Red, I know you wanted this bad, and I still believe that not all is lost; however, I think it's time we call off this witch hunt before the one person that actually does live here calls the one-man sheriff's office in this town and has the two of us arrested."

"Wait a minute. Before we leave, drive behind the garage just to see if we can spot anything that shows signs of them being here," Red requested.

"Red, I've known you for a real long time, and I respect you man, but I'm not feeling right about this. I think we need to leave."

"Fine then, wait right here," he said to Allen, quickly exiting the car and walking toward the back of the garage.

Red cautiously walked to the back side of the garage and noticed that, at some point, aside from being ground zero for an explosion, the garage was also a crime scene. He knew that being there as an outsider, snooping around, would make him easily identifiable in a lineup; or, even worse, accountable.

"The shop is closed, you foul-looking ginzo son of a bitch," a female voice called out to him, followed by the distinguishable sound of a shotgun being racked.

"I'm actually Irish."

"Same shit, different toilet bowl. What the hell do you want?" the woman angrily asked. "There's nothing here you can possibly want."

Red picked up on the apoplectic tone in her voice and knew that if he made the wrong move, he could be blown away; even worse, blown away from the back.

"Miss, I'm going to turn around, okay? So, don't shoot. I don't know what happened here, but I can assure you that I had nothing to do with it," Red nervously explained, hoping that he could buy some time to either defuse the situation while obtaining some information, or cause Allen to come check up on him, see that he was in a bad situation and blast the unstable woman.

"My name is Sean, but everyone calls me Red," he explained to her as he slowly turned. They were now face to face. "What's your name?"

"My name is 'I'm soon going to pull this trigger and get rid of your ass for snooping in these parts'. What the hell do you care what my name is?"

"I'm just looking for someone that could have come through here, but obviously this is not the place."

"Damn right this is not the place, so get your ass out of here before I blast it for trespassing!" she threatened him, never losing visual focus.

"Miss, you are absolutely right, and I am sorry to have bothered you. We'll be on our way."

"Red, what the fuck is going on?"

"No, Al, don't shoot!" Red screamed out as he saw Allen turn the corner of the garage, pointing his gun at the woman.

"Tell him to put it down," she yelled at Red, turning around and pointing her shotgun at Allen.

"Fuck her, Red, she's seen our faces. She has to go."

"No, Al, she's good. Stand down."

"Screw that shit, she's gotta go," Allen confrontationally yelled back.

As the hostile standoff increased in intensity, the rational ability to compromise deteriorated with every unblinking moment. Allen, Red and the unidentified woman remained silent as the cold winter air blew.

"Allen, she is of no harm to us," Red calmly explained after the several minutes of gazing at one another came to an end. The realization hit them that anyone shooting was the last thing any of them wanted.

"What do you want?" she asked Red, never losing focus on Allen.

"We're looking for some men that could have come here. We got this information from a business associate of ours in Chicago and it led us here," Red calmly explained to her.

"And who is this associate of yours?"

"Omar. Omar Lameda," Red reluctantly told her.

Her eyes, which revealed acknowledgment when she heard the name, allowed him to make the connection. Although time had allowed her to adapt to her environment, almost masking her true identity, her now-exposed Hispanic features revealed who she was.

"Do you know Omar?"

"I do. He is family, and more than likely responsible for all of this."

"How so?" Red asked as he motioned for Allen to drop his weapon.

"He sent some Puerto Rican guys down here to meet up with my husband, and then this happens," she answered, never dropping her shotgun.

"Did you get their names or how many of them there were?"

"What is this, a thousand questions? All I know is that they needed a vehicle or something like that."

"Did they say anything about where they were heading to?"

"Not sure. My husband mentioned something about a twin city, wherever the hell that's at. All I know is I was going to meet up with my husband and this shit happens. So, if you don't mind, I'm going to ask you one last time to get the hell off of my property," she said to Red as she closed one eye and focused on Allen, who was starting to make her nervous.

"I'm sorry for your loss, and I can assure you that we had nothing to do with whatever happened here, but you pointing that shotgun is starting to make us nervous, especially for my friend here. So, if you don't mind, I think I've found everything that was needed, and we'll make our way out of here," Red explained. He could see that her patience was slowly fading away.

"Yeah, I think that's best," she responded. She slowly walked around Red, allowing him to cautiously make his way toward Allen.

"You know, we can probably work together. I get to find what I'm looking for, and you get closure," he tried to reason with her.

"The only thing that will bring me closure is you getting the hell out of here," she sternly told him, followed by the sound of, what he believed was, her about to pull the trigger.

From the harsh winter that had been endlessly unforgiving, there were layers of packed snow that concealed buried ice just underneath Red and Allen's feet, making it difficult for them to maintain their balance. As they walked off, an unforeseen tree branch crash landed on the ground, causing the woman to impetuously react.

Red and Allen widened their eyes at what they were witnessing. Believing the distraught woman defensively pulled the trigger, they were forced to hit the ground in cover.

The sound of a shotgun echoed through the cold and desolate streets, forcing birds to fly away and wildlife alike to stop. Red and Allen, who were both face-first on the snow-covered ground, looked at each other, confirming neither one was shot, then turned their heads in her direction.

"Al, what the hell just happened?"

"I don't know, Red, but that yahoo is lying on the ground."

"Do you think she…" he began to question, but stopped himself when he saw a pool of blood expanding around her head as the smell of death filled the wintry air.

"Someone must have shot her," Red said as he scanned their surroundings for a potential shooter.

"I don't think so, Red. The bitch shot herself."

"Suicide?"

"Perhaps, I don't know," Allen immediately replied. "But there's only one way to find out, and I can assure you it's not going to happen by me sliding over there to confirm it," he said as he picked himself up from the cold snow that was breaching his slacks.

"Oh shit, I think she slipped on the ice and blasted herself in the head," Allen said in total shock.

"How is that even possible?"

"I don't know, Red, but if you think about, we didn't hear any shots fired from another direction. Not to mention, what we heard was a shotgun. Not a handgun or a rifle, but a damn shotgun."

"Damn, if that's true, what a way to go. She actually wasn't that bad looking."

"Red, the bitch blew half her fucking face off and all you can think about is how much of a piece of ass she was. You truly have fucking issues, my friend."

"That's not what I'm saying, Al, and you know it."

"Well, I don't care what the fuck you meant, but we better get the hell out of here before the local yahoos ride in on their snowmobiles, snooping around, thinking a neighbor shot some dinner."

"I guess you're right. Let's get the hell out of here," Red replied as he looked at his watch. "She mentioned twin cities."

"Red, there are a lot of places that call themselves twin cities. Places in Ohio, Indiana, Michigan; hell, even Minnesota has twin cities."

"Well, we better come up with a suitable choice fast," Red said to him. The idea of chasing his childhood friends across the country did not settle right with him.

"Superior, Wisconsin and Duluth, Minnesota—these sound like a good place to start," Red said out loud.

"So, let me get this straight, Red: What you are basically saying is, that faceless woman mentioned twin cities—which, in reality, can be in any city across this country—and now you want to head to the first twin city your phone came up with first?" replied Allen, watching Red search his phone.

"Do you have a problem with the location I picked, Al?"

Bravado Brothers

"Listen to me, Red. You're a good man, and if this works out for you, you're going to start your own family—which, by the way, I hope I would even be considered for a position in—but you know damn well I'm not going to debate anything with you, especially when it comes to a personal choice you've made about tracking your childhood comrades. However, this is like a needle in a haystack."

"I'm riding shotgun," said Red, dismissing Allen's observation.

* *

"This is a great place to start," Allen said to Red, who was looking at the tranquil street that led to a bridge.

Refusing to entertain Allen's sarcastic and truthful scrutiny, Red continued staring directly at a bridge that divided the cities of Superior, Wisconsin and Duluth, Minnesota. It was a location he felt would have allowed a person on the run to lay low. He was already tired of traveling, being cooped up in a car, eating fast food and losing vital sleep.

Leaning his head back and caressing his face to release some tension, he replied to Allen with a tolerant demeanor, "For your information, this bridge we're parked at will allow us to quickly cross over from one part of town in one state to another. I picked this location, if you must know, because small towns like these are ideal for hiding out. You can also easily generate local revenue, mainly in the numbers business, which, by the way, these guys are really good at."

"But Red, there is absolutely nothing around here. I mean, we're at a gas station, across the street from a steakhouse—which, by the way, I have not seen one person go into—and some low budget hotel. Not to mention, there's like minimal traffic out here."

"Well, whether you like it or not, this is our first location. So do me a favor, stop with the skepticism and keep your ears and eyes open. In some form or another, you have worked with all these guys in the past. You know what they look like, sound like, and how cautious they are; and believe me when I tell you, they will have no issues taking you out if they feel you are a threat—which, by the way, you are," Red replied.

"Well, since we're already here, can we go to this steakhouse? I'm starving and if I eat one more hotdog or burger from a gas station, I'm going to lose it. I am not joking, Red."

"Yeah, I guess you're right. We might as well get some rooms while we're here because I'm all disoriented. Not to mention, I haven't taken a peaceful shit or bathed for a few days now."

"I hope they have good steaks there because there is nothing worse than eating a shitty steak at a steakhouse," Allen said as he looked at himself in the rearview mirror, straightening his hair.

"What the hell are you fixing yourself for? It's not like we're going to Gibson's or any of those places back home," Red said, unlocking the door and getting ready to exit.

"True, but when you go into a steakhouse looking like you're not there to enjoy the ambiance or tip the waiter, the cooks give you the side of the beef that the cow was laying on."

"You know something, Al, you're right. I better fart in here instead of blasting one inside the restaurant," Red replied as he lifted one leg out of the car and shredded a hellacious fart that ejected Allen out immediately.

Like two strangers in a strange land, Red and Allen audaciously walked the desolate street in Superior, Wisconsin, in pursuit of their intended targets. Unfamiliar with their territory, they casually enter the antiquated steakhouse and smiled at the smells of fresh bread baking, musty alcohol and searing steak on the grill.

They instinctively observed the restaurant, which only had a few patrons quietly enjoying their evening meal, and were startled when a female voice crept up behind them and welcomed them to the humble establishment.

"How you boys doing?"

Allen, who hated anyone approaching him from behind, turned away so that he would refrain from lashing out at the hostess. After all, she did not know.

"Thank you, miss. If you don't mind, we'll head to the bar for a couple of drinks and then some of your well-known steaks," he replied to her realizing that Allen was about to lash out. As they walked to the bar, he turned to Allen and said,

"What the hell is the matter with you? You're getting your panties all in a wad over a hostess from a town most of America has never heard of?"

"Sorry, Red, I spent so many years working on the force and dealing with low-lives from the streets, I guess I still haven't moved past that."

"Well, you're no longer a cop. You were hired by Mr. Levine to help me because of your expertise, so do me a favor, and calm the fuck down. Not everyone is a criminal!" Red sternly whispered to him as they both sat down at the end of the bar, allowing them to view anyone walking in.

"Two pints, two Jim Beams," Red ordered.

"I'm not a big Bourbon-Whiskey drinker," Allen explained to Red, showing a dislike for the order.

"Who the hell said I ordered for the two of us?" Red replied, looking at the female bartender.

"I'll just have a pint," Allen ordered as he noticed a couple of deputy sheriffs entering the steakhouse.

Red and Allen, who had turned their attention toward the television above the bar mirror, slightly looked at each other, smiled and picked up the menu to avoid any eye contact with Superior's finest.

"I wonder how the ham sandwiches are here," Allen commented to Red, using the code for a dirty cop. Allen had flashed the badge for about twelve years before realizing that there was more money to be made outside the structured remuneration. He could easily spot cops on the take.

"Are you sure?" Red questioned.

"Are you kidding me? Do you honestly believe that these meat eaters earn a decent living here, whatever you call this place? I bet you that these poor folks have to pay to watch their beloved Packers on T.V. Fuck yeah, they are."

Like two turkey vultures anticipating meal time, Allen and Red monitored the deputies entering the kitchen and, shortly after, witnessed a patrol car exiting the parking lot from the front window.

"So, we're in Packers territory, huh?" Allen asked the bartender, who was dusting the bottles behind the bar.

"You betcha," she politely responded, albeit with a frustrated look which caught their attention.

"So, is there a sports bar around here where someone can go and watch several games? Perhaps place some bets if they wanted to?"

The bartender, who immediately gave Allen a suspicious look, grabbed the bottle of Jim Beam to refill Red's drink.

"This is a small town, so betting here is almost nonexistent. However, if that is the sort of thing you're into, you can always go over the bridge and place your bets there. There's a small town casino there," she replied with a forced smile.

Red, who picked up on her incivility, was laughing on the inside as he watched Allen cease his inquiry due to the intrusive awkwardness.

Allen knew that she was not going to reveal much, and in so many words was saying to back off. He swiveled away from her, stood up, drank the remaining beer from his mug, removed his jacket, placed it on the back of the stool, looked at Red and stated loudly: "If I wanted that kind of disrespect, I'd go hump on my ex-wife and ask her if it was good."

"Sorry, my friend doesn't mean any disrespect," Red explained to her as he watched Allen walk toward the restroom.

With a questionable stare, and a smile that Red perceived as disingenuous, she refilled Allen's drink, placed it on the coaster and turned to Red. Placing both of her hands on the counter, she told him: "Don't take this the wrong way, but we get a lot of outsiders coming through these doors, looking for a small town like ours to plant their operations."

"Miss, I mean no disrespect—and yes, we are just passing by—but all we want is a few drinks, hopefully some good steaks, and, while we're here, we're looking for some associates of ours that perhaps made their home here."

"You see, this is what I am talking about," she responded.

"Whoa, whoa, whoa. I think you've got us all confused."

"No, I don't," she cut him off. "You city grease balls come here with your fancy city looks and your menacing mannerisms, and you come here to rob these innocent, hardworking folks of their hard-earned living."

"Look, I can assure you that we do not want to make any trouble. All we are doing is looking for some men," he explained to her with a straight face. "Have you ever seen these men before?" He pulled out some recent pictures from a wedding of the five of them.

"Is everything alright, Maggie?" an authoritative voice, coming from behind Red, asked her.

But the bartender, whose eyes widened, did not answer as she backed away from the bar.

Red immediately looked in the mirror behind the bar and saw a law enforcement officer standing behind him, pointing a shiny, silver pistol at his head.

"We don't want any trouble here," the bartender, now identified as Maggie, told Allen, who was back from the bathroom and got the drop on the officer.

"Fuck, Allen, I had everything under control."

"Really? It sure doesn't look that way," Allen replied as he pointed his pistol at the officer, who began lowering his service weapon.

"Please, we have young ones at home and we want no trouble," Maggie explained to Red, revealing that she and the officer were married.

Red placed his hands on the back of his neck, looked at Allen and said, "Whatever you do, do not shoot these folks."

"Well, in case you haven't noticed, it's not like I have much of a choice," Allen responded.

"Please, we want no trouble."

"Shut the fuck up," Allen calmly told her. "You mentioned that already."

Red noticed some patrons enjoying dinner on the other side of the restaurant, separated by a wall and currently unaware of the circumstances at the bar. He knew he had to swiftly react, for time was not on his and Allen's side.

"Deputy, hand me your radio and the keys to your patrol car—and if you hit that orange button on your radio, your children will be fatherless," Allen commanded.

"Where is your freezer?" Red asked the bartender.

"It's…it's…"

"Shh," Red motioned to her with his finger over his lips, attempting to calm her down.

With her finger uncontrollably shaking, she pointed toward the back.

"Is there anyone back there?" Red calmly asked her.

"No."

"What do you mean 'no'?" he asked, glancing at the back, hoping he could pick up on some movement.

"My cooks aren't scheduled to come in until thirty minutes from now," she explained.

"Who the fuck has been cooking, then?" Allen asked her, for they smelled food being cooked throughout the restaurant.

"I'm the cook," the deputy told them.

"Are you serious?" Red asked as he looked at Allen, who, not long ago, explained to him about officers in small towns.

"You're joking, right?" Red asked again, looking the deputy up and down, from head to toe, inspecting his uniform.

"In case you haven't noticed, not much is happening now. But soon, many will come and I promise you, your asses are mine."

"Whoa, whoa, whoa, no need to get hostile here, officer," Allen said as he tried to read the unusual name on the officer's tag.

"Another thing you can do is call me 'deputy'—it's pretty obvious you don't know the difference," he sarcastically said to Allen, who sported an indifferent smirk.

"You know, normally I would just blast a person's face off for stupid comments like that; but you have balls, and I like that, so this is what I'm going to do."

* *

With frozen steaks duct taped around his head and cheeks, the deputy's arms were pulled back and handcuffed around his wife's stomach. She was struggling to suppress her gag reflex from her mouth being stuffed with sausage, as she was secured with duct tape to the freezer pole. Allen stood on the opposite side of the pole and sported an irremovable grin as he sadistically admired his workmanship. He rubbed his hands together as the cold, frigid air in the meat locker started numbing his fingers.

"Al, this is some sick shit."

"What, you never placed people in a meat locker before?"

"No, not that, but stuffing sausage in her mouth? That's a blatant disrespect," replied Red as he grabbed his coat, ready to leave.

"A blatant disrespect? Are you kidding me?" Allen responded, walking over to the deputy. He turned his attention to the deputy, "Hey, law man, that's some talent that wife of yours has. Where I come from, we call her a keeper."

Allen looked over at Red, who was shaking his head in disbelief.

"Oh, and one more thing: the nipples on your wife…wow. She can scratch the paint off a car with those things," Allen taunted him as he and Red walked out of the freezer and closed the door behind them.

"Alright, before we leave, we need to ditch that patrol car, perhaps behind the gas station. Believe me, it will take them several days to find it, buying us some time to go to this so-called casino and snoop around," Allen explained while looking at the reflection of the cruiser's window and adjusting his sheriff's baseball cap.

"You're a sick son of a bitch for wearing the man's hat."

"Wearing this hat brings me back, I tell you."

"But you were never a deputy sheriff, you were police."

"Same pig, different barn, Red."

"Well I tell you what, Mr. Pig, let's get out of here before someone decides to actually have dinner at the only restaurant in town. The idea that there's no traffic of any kind in this town freaks me the hell out," Red said to him as he looked around, amazed by the minimal amount of human activity.

Chapter XIV

A Casino In The Rough

"What the hell is this place?" Red commented to Allen as they slowly drove to what looked like a department store or a nightclub.

"Oh, sausage mouth over at the restaurant did mention to go over the bridge and place our bets. I guess she meant this casino," Allen replied.

"If this is a casino, why isn't this neighborhood crowded with people?" Red asked, watching small clusters of people enter and exit the building.

"Maybe they're all inside," Allen suggested, his face lit up from the outside neon lights that were flickering on and off. He pointed out, "Well, there are some folks walking the street and exiting the casino."

"True, but those are locals."

"How do you know?" Allen asked, questioning Red's observation.

"Because they all have that yokel Midwest look to them."

"Shit, Red, you're right. I wonder what they say about us."

"What do you mean? We look fine."

"Oh yeah, I guess you're right. Like the way we entered that bar and were accepted as equals with the locals," Allen sarcastically said as he parked the car, just walking distance from the casino.

"It was the line of questioning that raised red flags, not the way we were dressed."

"Really, Red…is that what you're going with? The line of questioning?" Allen asked with a raised eyebrow.

"Well, it's true," Red replied as he looked in the visor mirror to straighten his hair.

"That is the biggest crock of shit I have ever heard. What makes that statement even more pathetic, is that you actually believe that bullshit," Allen shot back.

The two checked their chambers inside their pistols and exited the vehicle.

With a hesitant walk that displayed unfamiliarity, Red and Allen, oblivious to their environment, aimlessly entered the vibrant and loud casino that was occupied by attentive gamblers from all walks of life.

The casino was impressively clean, energetic and visually engaging. It surprised both Red and Allen, who were taken aback by the casino's abundance of tables and slot machines, and the extravagant bar that was continuously in demand.

"This might be a place where they would find it suitable to establish a relationship and set up shop," Red commented to Allen, finding himself mesmerized by all the women serving drinks; they all had an unusual look to them.

"So, what do you think?"

"I don't know, Red. These are your people and you know how they operate. Would they consider a place like this?"

"I'm not sure."

"Would you?" Allen asked Red, as he also stared at the barmaids' uniquely unusual look."

"Hey, Red, I don't mean to change the subject, but are these woman Spanish? Or are they Greek?"

"I'm not sure, but there is something unusual about them," Red replied as he scoped out the casino, hoping he could get a visual on any of childhood friends.

"So, can I get you gentlemen a drink?" a barmaid asked them when she noticed that they were the only two in the casino not playing.

"Yeah, sure, let me get a Jim Beam," Red requested.

"Make that two," Allen ordered, looking deep into the barmaid's eyes.

"I'll be right back gentleman, and hopefully you will be at a table or yanking on a lever," she indirectly suggested.

"Oh, we will, we're just admiring the scenery. The layout of this casino is misleading—in a good way, of course," Red courteously commented.

"Granted, it's not Vegas. But, for a small town in Duluth, Minnesota, it serves its purpose," she said, picking up on his insincerity. "I'll be right back."

After several minutes of observing the casino environment, keeping an eye out for anyone who possibly provided gambling outside the gaming house, the barmaid returned with their drinks and smiled at the two of them.

"I see you gentlemen found a nice little table—I wish you luck tonight. The drinks are on the house for as long as you are playing. My name is Lala and I will be sure to come by to check up on the two of you."

"Thank you, Lala, and maybe later you can tell us where a person can perhaps place some bets outside this fine establishment," Red said as he placed a twenty dollar bill on her small, round serving tray.

"Well, all the betting you need is right in here," she replied.

"What I meant was, you know, like betting on sporting events—you know, like Vegas."

"Well, I don't know of any person that does anything like that here, but enjoy your visit here today," she dismissively replied to him before she walked away and disappeared within the sea of gamblers.

"Red, something isn't right. I don't know what it is, but she and this place are leaving me with strange vibes. I mean, look at the barmaids—they all kind of look alike. And the security here, it's like they're all related. I just can't put my finger on it."

"Yeah, I'm feeling that too. Tell you what, let's just hang around for a short while, see if there are any signs of Sebastian or the others, and then get the hell out of here. I'm sure that our friends cooling in that meat locker over at Superior have been found, and finding us will be their top priority."

"Shit, I forgot about them," Allen replied with a laugh.

"Well, let's laugh about that later and focus on finding these guys and getting the hell out of here before there's a bolo out on us," Red said as he started noticing some of the workers looking at them.

"Do yourselves a favor, and don't make any sudden moves or scream like a little village whore," a male voice whispered behind Red's ear.

In all his years of encountering law enforcement and criminals alike, never had Red heard anyone threaten them with terms like, 'scream like a little village whore.'

"Did I not tell you to not make any sudden moves?" the man asked, prohibiting Red from turning around to look at his assailant.

Allen remained quiet and just smiled at the man flashing a silver pistol behind Red. He knew they got caught sleeping.

"Alright, slick, I need for you to turn around, start walking toward the bar and push open the door. We're all going to get to know each other," the unknown man told Allen.

"Do you know who we are?" Red calmly asked the man behind him as he was led to the door behind the bar.

"Who you are really doesn't concern me, and it's not important. Who wants to speak to you, is," he replied to Red as he led him into a narrow stairway that was minimally lit, cold and musty.

Red and Allen were met by two large, bearded individuals who forced them to turn around and scanned them with a metal detector. "I don't think the two of you will be needing these," one of the men said, removing Red and Allen's guns.

"Alright, assholes, I will only explain this to you one time: Remove everything from your pockets and place them inside the bag."

Red and Allen, who understood that any type of resistance on their part could cost them their lives, calmly began removing all the contents from their pockets.

"Alright, you two can turn around now," they were instructed. "I am a man of very little patience, so please don't make me repeat myself to the two of you. When you get upstairs, don't say anything until spoken to. Don't laugh, don't smile and don't frown—nothing. Do the two of you understand me?" a tall medium build man explained.

Both Red and Allen felt, for the first time, that they were potentially in an uncompromising position, and so refrained from any hostile commentary that would have jeopardized their life. Instead, they simply nodded in compliance and began walking up a narrow flight of steps that was carpeted with dated designs and unwelcoming colors that immediately altered there mood.

"Remember, don't test my patience and everything will be alright," they were reminded as they were lead to an office.

"Come in, come in, and welcome to our Casino. My name is Tawno Marks, and you are...excuse me, where are my manners? Would you like a drink, or perhaps would like one of my people to make you two a plate?" he politely offered.

"No, we're good," Red replied, glancing at the photos and paintings of women with headscarves, horse wagons, and crystal balls.

"Are you sure? Because my guys are trained to observe our guests out on the floor, and they tell me that you two looked like you were not having a good time. Perhaps even a little confused about your surroundings," he said as he looked at a wall filled with monitors showing camera shots of the casino floor.

"It's our first time here and we were just admiring the casino," Red replied.

"Understood. So, what are your names?"

"My name is Red, and this is my associate, Allen."

"Is that really your name? What, did your mother not like you? And were neither of you given last names?" he asked them as he opened up their wallets that were handed to him by his security.

"Well, that's what they call me—"

"Give me a second," he interrupted Red. He removed his glasses from his shirt pocket and looked at their driver's licenses.

"Well, according to this, your name is Sean McLoughlin, not Red, and you are Allen Morrison. Did I disrespect you in any way? Did I not introduce myself respectfully?"

"Mr. Marks, we meant no disrespect—"

"I was talking to Mr. Sean here," he cut off Allen, never losing eye contact with Red.

"So, as you were about to explain to me."

"We meant no disrespect. My friends and family call me Red—"

"So, what you are saying is that I am a friend? Wow, I feel honored. So, please, go on."

"As I was about to explain, my friends and family call me Red, but my full name is Sean McLoughlin."

"Now, was that so difficult?" he said Red, before turning his attention to Allen. "Your turn now."

"My name is Allen Morrison and you have a fine establishment here."

Tawno Marks' thunderous laugh silenced the whole room. In his composed demeanor, he snapped his fingers twice and was handed a small glass filled with liquor.

"So, Mr. Sean and Mr. Allen, the two of you are a long way from home. What brings you to Duluth?"

"We're just passing by, looking for some old friends," Red replied.

"Perhaps I can help you? What are the names of these friends of yours?"

With a blank stare that revealed hesitation, Red straightened his shirt, forged a smile and told Tawno, "The friends I'm looking for, I doubt you know any of them, but their names are Sebastian and Fabian Rodriquez."

Red watched Tawno's face, hoping he could pick up on any expressions that would indicate an association.

"So, these friends that you seek require very large caliber pistols?"

"No, not really, but you never know," Allen replied, devoid of emotion.

"A man that does not know his own journey is a lost man."

"Is there a reason why we were brought here against our will, Mr. Marks?" Red sharply asked.

"Yes, there is," he sternly replied. He stood up from his desk chair and, with the palm of his hand, smacked the desk, causing his security to defensively react.

"You come to my place, asking for bookies and side beating services, and you think that nobody is going to ask questions? Either you don't give a shit, or you're just outrageously stupid."

"Mr. Marks, I apologize for coming into your establishment asking questions that might have sounded like we were trying to muscle in, but I can assure you that we are here to find these men. And if you know who they are and where we can find them, it might just benefit you," Red explained, showing no fear of their predicament.

"Well, I can assure you that I couldn't care less about anything that has to do with your manhunt, but you should have left this establishment when you had the chance, especially with what took place in Superior," he replied to Red. "What, you thought nobody was going to find those poor, hardworking folks you guys stuffed in the freezer? Not very smart, by the way."

"We had nothing to do with that," Allen responded.

"Really? Two never-before-seen out-of-towners walk into a beloved steakhouse and shortly after, a patrol car was driven by two non-law enforcement officers—which, by the way, took a lot of balls—who parked the car just a block away. This wasn't going to raise any suspicion? Did you really think nobody would have noticed any of this?"

Red and Allen, who could not respond, look at each other in disbelief.

"I know, I know. The whole 'nobody in the streets or in the steakhouse' thing led you two idiots to believe that no one would notice. Well, I guess you were fucking wrong," he yelled loudly as he stood up, pulled out Allen's pistol and pointed it at his head.

"Do you know who I am?" Allen asked him with a serious face.

"Am I supposed to?"

"I have killed more men in one year than you have in a lifetime. As a matter of fact, you have pussy written all over your eyes."

"For a man that has a gun pointed at his head, you sure speak boldly."

"It took me some time to figure you out; however, with all these silly photos and that shit English that you speak, it all makes sense now," Allen said, never flinching with fear.

"Well, tell me what makes sense," Tawno asked with a chuckle.

"For the longest time, the Romans, the Greeks, and even the ancient Japanese and Koreans had a whole lot of incest going on. However, with all that we now know when it comes to the harmful effects of breading from within, there are still some cultures today that don't know the difference and have never evolved," Allen methodically explained to him. "One of them is the hillbillies, and the other is the Gypsies. I mean, that's just common knowledge; and from the looks of you guys, it's pretty safe to assume that none of you are hillbillies."

Tawno's look of disbelief caused a chain reaction of outrage among those who were in the affluent office just above the casino. The co-owner and number two man in the family operation and organization remained too shocked from Allen's offensive commentary to speak until his phone rang.

"Hello?" Tawno answered.

"Mmmhhhhmmm...Mmmhhhhmmm...How long?"

He ended the call and turned to his main bodyguard as he made his way to the door. "Jardani, come with me. And if either of them move the wrong way, shoot them both in the head," Tawno shouted out in his Romanesque language before storming out.

Bravado Brothers

Ten Minutes Later

"Well, it's nice to see you again, Mr. Marks. I was starting to believe you were never going to come back," Allen said to him with a gun pointed at the barmaid's head, while Red finished tying up the last of Tawno's crew.

Tawno, shocked to see that Allen and Red had managed to remove themselves from their predicament, smiled and slowly sat on his chair.

"If I were you, I would teach your men, or whoever these folks are to you, proper searching technique," Allen continued. "They completely overlooked a small pistol in my front waistline. And, by the way, you are a smoking hot woman," he complimented the barmaid. "I had no idea you guys could turn out so beautiful." He finished his speech by viciously slapping her, sending her tumbling over a small bar table.

"Whoa, whoa, whoa, not so fast sheik," Red warned Tawno, who made to move. "She struck my friend here in the back of the head. You really need to get your women in check."

"Good luck with that," Tawno replied. "You're not going to make it very far, my friend."

"Ahh, we're back to being friends again," Red shot back. "Not long ago you told your chuck wagon comrades here to shoot us if we moved the wrong way."

"What do you want?"

"Allen, do you hear this fucking guy? We told you why we're here, but you didn't want to listen to us."

"Well, it doesn't matter anymore because the authorities are coming."

"You see, this is really confusing to me. First, you ask us what is that we want; then, when we explain it to you, you dismiss us. It's insulting, if you ask me," Red replied as he walked toward the window facing the casino.

"You will not make it far."

"I beg to differ, you smelly, hairy fuck. Hey, Allen, is it me or do these people have an unusual scent?" he asked as he pointed his gun away from Tawno, leading him to accidentally shoot one of the men who was tied up.

"You see what you made me do?" Red asked Tawno with a smile.

"I will search the ends of the earth and make sure you suffer a thousand deaths, you shit-eating Irish pig.

"You know something, under normal circumstances, a remark like that would have set me off, but coming from you and your species, it just doesn't have any substance. I will say this, however: An operation like this could have materialized into a prosperous business alliance, but now, it's all going to shit," Red explained to him. He stopped at the sound of footsteps from several people who were ready to breach the door.

"Allen?"

"I got it, Red."

"You have got to be kidding me. These are the authorities you were talking about?" Red loudly questioned, smiling at the sheriff's deputy from the steakhouse and the man named Jardani.

"You sons of bitches," the sheriff's deputy yelled out, looking around the room and seeing everyone tied up and the one barmaid palming her face.

"Well, unless you have an army coming this way, we will be parting ways. However, there is one last thing that needs to be done."

The Getaway

"Mr. Marks, don't take this the wrong way, but this could have turned out really bad. Instead, you'll be walking out of here alive; cold, but alive," Red said as he watched Allen lace the final knot, which prohibited the sheriff's deputy to detach from Tawno's backside.

"Al, you have some sick shit going on in your head. And by the way, do you think you have enough duct tape around his mouth?"

"Fuck 'em. If it were up to me they all would have received one in the head," Allen replied.

"I know, but to do all this, and in the freezer again—I mean, it's a lot of work, Al."

"Yeah, I guess you're right. But there is a silver lining to all of this."

"How the hell so?"

"What, are you kidding me? Look at the fucking nipples on her! They're driving me crazy—you can freaking cut glass with those things," he pointed out to Red and pulled down her low-cut shirt to expose her protruding nipples.

"Don't worry honey, a rapist I am not. However, there is no way I wasn't going to look at them," Allen told her.

"And what's up with all the sausage stuffed in these women's months?"

"Well, think about Red: If she's good—and something tells me that she is—she'll slowly eat it all."

"But she has duct tape over her lips."

"Hey, law man, did your wife get to eat that sausage? That's what I fucking thought," Allen said as the deputy mumbled out in anger.

"Alright, alright, don't get your panties all in a wad. Let's go, Red, before someone decides they need to come in this extremely large freezer. This place is starting to get packed."

"Alright, Tawno, this is the deal: We have your phones, your wallets, and your guns. What I am going to do is quietly walk out. I'll make a call from your cell about an hour from now and will let one of your people know where all of you can be found," Red explained. "That is, of course, if we don't run into trouble before we leave. But I don't think that's going to happen. Do you understand me? Good. Good luck, you."

Chapter XV

Panting From The Skirmish

"When are you planning on coming back?" Khan angrily asked over the phone as he paced back and forth.

"Sebastian, I'm telling you that this is getting out of hand. All he does is brings home these mammoth-sized freaking women every night, and I tell you, it's fucking disturbing. The laughing, the moaning; and then he has the audacity to invite me into that pigpen as if I was even fucking interested. Sebastian, it's not funny. Wait a minute…"

Khan held the phone down and listened to the sounds in the apartment.

"Sorry, I thought I heard them walk out of the bedroom. Sebastian, I love my brother, I love my family, but I cannot do this anymore. Last night after working late at the restaurant, I had to go to the market because we're low on food again. I purchased, as I always do, six pounds worth of cold cuts so that we can have something to eat in the morning, and all of it is gone. What the fuck!" he yelled out in frustration. He walked into the next room, watched someone exit the bedroom, and continued talking to Sebastian over the phone,

"Oh my god, that fat blonde one—you know, the one he really likes that's here like two to three times a week—is walking toward the kitchen naked."

"Fabe, there's no more!" the blonde woman yelled out.

"Sebastian, if you are not here by tomorrow night, I am going to get in the car and I am heading back to Chicago. I will take my chances," Khan whispered into the phone, hoping he would not be heard.

"Khan, where's all the food, man?"

"Sebastian, Fabian is right in front of me, naked, swinging his dick in my face. I am not fucking with you anymore. Get your ass over here, now!" he yelled and hung up the phone.

"Fabian, what the fuck do you want?!"

"Khan, what the hell? Why are you all freaked out?"

"What the hell is it, Fabe?" Khan asked again, looking away from his brother.

"Dude, what the hell? All I want to know is what happened to all the food that was in the fridge. Did we not stock up just days ago?"

"You and those freaking wide-mouth, food-gobbling, orca-looking bitches that you bring here every night—"

"Who the hell are you calling orca you little-dick Chinese motherfucker," the blonde yelled out to Khan in a threatening manner.

"Whoa, whoa, whoa. That's my brother, watch what you're saying," Fabian intervened.

"Yeah, I'm his brother. And for your information, I'm Vietnamese, you fucking giant-size, sumo-looking bitch!"

"I will kick your ass, you little son of a bitch," she yelled out, rushing forward to take Khan down.

Fabian, who was six feet in height and weighed around two hundred and ten pounds, was no match for the plus-size, former collegiate tug-of-war champion. As he struggled to hold her back, he said,

"Angela, get dressed and we'll go out to eat. Khan, when I'm done I will personally go to the market and buy us some groceries, and when I get back we'll go to work, okay?"

"Fine, but you better replace all the cold cuts she ate in one sitting," Khan yelled out as he slammed his bedroom door behind him.

Fabian, panting from the skirmish, walked over to the refrigerator to grab a cold drink. When he looked inside, to his astonishment, he realized that Khan had a valid argument.

Bravado Brothers

Element of Surprise

"What's up, Freddy? How are you doing?" Fabian greeted the restaurant owner were they ran their illegal numbers and bookie operation.

"I'm well, Fabian."

"Where's my brother?" Fabian asked, looking at the booth they all usually sat at which was currently occupied by other patrons."

"He's in the kitchen."

"He's in the kitchen? Like what, preparing food or something?"

"Fabian, all he said was, when you get here, to make sure and tell you to go through the back, quietly. Fabian, he's acting kind of weird; please, I don't want any trouble here."

"I know this is your place, and none of us want any trouble, so just know all is good," Fabian assured him.

"Look, you guys have been very good to me, and I appreciate the business and payouts, but Khan has not moved from that spot since he's been here and he's not saying a word. He's been looking at these two guys sitting outside the lounge for well over an hour," Freddy whispered to him. He continued explaining in a reasonable voice,

"Fabian, I don't want any shit here. It's Sunday, and we've worked hard to promote the restaurant's family-friendly atmosphere. These are families that just came from church and all they want is a chill meal in a family environment. So do me a favor, if there is anything that's unusual, just leave and conduct your business tomorrow when things are a little calmer."

"You know that we appreciate our arrangement and would never compromise it," Fabian assured him as he shook his hand and walked away to approach Khan.

"Khan, why are you wearing a chef's hat? Are you cooking today, testing your culinary skills?"

"No, you dumbass. I'm looking at these two jerk-offs sitting outside, not ordering anything but Cokes," Khan snapped at him.

"Yeah, so?"

"Fabian, it never astonishes me how, time after time, you manage to overlook pertinent information in your life; simple stuff like faces, names, and locations."

"Khan, are you still upset about the cold cuts? I replaced it all, for your information."

"No, I'm not upset about the cold cuts. I mean, watching that behemoth of a woman walk naked in our living room was disturbing; but upset about the cold-cuts? No. It's to be expected."

"Okay, sorry that I even asked. So, I come in looking for you, and Freddy is a little concerned about you scoping out two men during a very busy time at his restaurant."

"Why didn't he just come up to me?"

"Khan, something tells me that he has. So, what is it about these two that I should know?"

"I remember Avvi would, from time to time, use two guys to collect large sums of money when it came to collecting outside the state. He would use them because they were good at tracking folks. I'm not one hundred percent sure, but I think these are those same guys."

"What are you saying, Khan? That these are the guys who were hired to track us?"

"I don't know, but them being here strictly by coincidence is not sitting well with me. I'm trying to remember their names, but I'm drawing a blank."

"So, what do you want to do?" Fabian asked as he started studying their characteristics.

"I don't know, but them just sitting there, ordering Cokes is driving me crazy."

"I know what to do," Fabian said as he pulled out his phone. "Angela is working out on the floor right now. I'm going to text her and have her approach these two and see if she can get them to order something, just to get a feel for them."

"She works here?"

"Khan, are you serious? She's been working here for well over a year now. How is it even possible that you didn't recognize her?"

"Fabe, all your girlfriends look alike. Fat and hungry."

"Let me tell you something, one day you're going to say the wrong thing about them and I'm not going to be able to stop them from hurting you. Look what happened today. Just imagine if I hadn't been there."

"Fabe, just tell her to do it," Khan said to him as frustration started settling in.

"So, are you boys ready to order or do you need more time?" Angela pleasantly asked the two men drinking Cokes.

"No, I think we're going to be leaving."

"I'm sorry, was the service bad? Is there something I can do?"

"I believe we might be in the wrong place."

"Well, if you're looking for steaks, you came to the right place. We have a selection that's been worthy of praise by many of the food critics in the city. They have, time after time, given us great reviews," she explained.

"I'm sure the food is fine here, but what we seek is not served here. We're looking for a specialty place where one can go and get an array of martinis and the atmosphere is much more catered, if you know what I mean," one of the men replied to her with a wink.

"Ahhh, I see. Well, I shouldn't be recommending any other places to our patrons, however, there is a place on University Avenue that might be more of a suitable environment. It's called Scallywags. Here's the address," she said to them as she pulled out her pen and started writing the name and address.

"Thank you. How much for the Cokes?"

"It's okay—on the house."

"Well, here. For you troubles and understanding."

"No trouble at all," she replied as she graciously smiled at the fifty dollar bill she received as a tip before heading back to the kitchen.

"So, what did they say? Why did they leave?" Fabian asked with a confused look.

"Well, if you must know, those two burly men are gay."

"What the hell do you mean 'they're gay'?"

"They're gay, just like I said."

"What makes you say that?" Fabian asked, looking at Khan uncertainly.

"Well, they mentioned that they're looking for a specialty place that serves an assortment of martinis."

"Really, that's it? That makes them gay?"

"Do you know how many people have come through these doors? Not one of them has ever ordered martinis or handed me a fifty for my troubles. Straight men, men with families, don't ever tip that way. Only gay men, and I love them."

"I don't get it. How can they be gay?" Fabian questioned, still not accepting her explanation.

"What is there not to get? I mean, look at you two. You're asking about two guys and why they're not ordering—what's it to you? And Fabe, don't get me wrong, I love you, especially how you ride me in so many ways, but let's consider some facts here: You are good looking, well-built for your age, you've never married, and don't have children. If you ask me that has fag written all over it."

Khan, who glanced at the man he had only known as his brother, wondered if her observation held any truth.

"And you, Khan: You are as soft-looking as they come. I mean, today I was naked in front of you and you didn't respond. I'm willing to bet that if I had a schlong, you would have considered it," she said to him.

Fabian found her commentary all too amusing and grabbed Khan's ass.

"Look, I have to get to work. Will I see you again sometime this week?"

"I don't know, I have to ask my man first," Fabian sarcastically replied before kissing her and walking her out.

"Fabian, I had no idea that I would have considered myself that way. Well, at least it's comforting to know that she doesn't know anything about us."

"Why would I tell her anything about us?"

"Fabe, you ride these woman as if they were elephants in Thailand. It's absolutely disturbing, and you telling them intimate details about us would not surprise me."

"Khan, what is it with you and the women I bring home?"

"I'm sorry, did my complaint come off as personal in nature? Because I can assure you that I am not the only one that feels this way."

"Screw you, Khan."

"Maybe I was wrong, maybe these aren't the guys I was thinking of. There's no way they could be gay," Khan said. The idea of mistaking the two men for hitmen troubled him.

"Well, nothing surprises me anymore," Fabian replied. "But if they are going to be a problem, I'm sure it will come up again."

"Yeah, I guess you're right," Khan replied, uncertain.

Chapter XVI

Out-Of-Towners

"So, there have been, as of late, some large bets placed in our network. With that being said, those very same large bets have been winners," Adam, explained. He, Frankie, Fabian, Sebastian, and Khan were all sitting at a round table, counting money and organizing betting slips.

"What are we talking about here, large payouts?" Sebastian asked.

"Substantial. Enough to put us back if these folks in particular continue with their little winning streak...or if anyone wins, for that matter."

"So, what are you saying? That we shouldn't take their bets anymore?" Sebastian questioned.

"Well, if we do that, word might get around that we're becoming sore losers, and that's not good for business."

"Frankie, did you know about this?" Sebastian asked.

"No, I didn't. Besides, people are going to win."

"Well, shouldn't you know about these things?" Khan jumped in. "I mean, you're like the muscle, right?"

"I got your muscle right here, Khan," Frankie replied as he grabbed his crotch, igniting the room with roaring laughter.

"Do you know who they are?" Sebastian asked. The idea of losing large sums of money to pay off a gambling debt needed to be addressed.

"Not really sure. One of our guys, the one we just hired to work for us on Wednesdays while we collect, was who received their tickets."

"You think we're getting played?"

"I don't think so, but if we continue getting hit like this, our personal payroll will be reduced."

"Bring your guy in here so that we that we can ask him some questions," Frankie told Adam, cocking his pistol.

"What's that for? You going to shoot the guy now?" Fabian asked as he continued counting money.

"If I pick up on anything that says he was in on this, lights out."

"Well, don't shoot him over the money," Sebastian agreeably said.

Adam walked back in with the newest member of the operation. "So, before we get started, let me introduce you to the crew: This is Sebastian, Fabian and their brother Khan; and you already know my cousin Frankie. Fellas, this is Mickey," Adam formally introduced the young bet collector.

"So, Mickey, what's your full name?" Khan asked, showing little interest as he continued counting the money laid out on the table.

"Michael Hersch."

"Hersch? What is that, Jewish?"

"Just the name," he responded, observing everyone's bland facial expressions.

"What, you're not proud of who you are?" Fabian asked as he got up from the table and walked toward the wet bar to make himself a drink.

"I am, however, when you explain to people—especially from the upper Midwest—that you're Jewish, they often respond with prejudice."

"Well, you don't have to feel that way here. I speak Spanish, was raised Catholic and I can assure you that I know the feeling," Khan explained to him, breaking the peculiarity of their introduction.

"Well, Mickey, the reason we called you up here is because Adam tells us that you've been doing a great job pooling customers together. Believe me when I tell you that we are grateful—it's hard to find people who are approachable and know the game," Sebastian told him with a straight face.

"Thank you, and I'm happy to be working here, but I feel this is more than a formal introduction," Mickey responded.

"Well, Mickey, it's been brought to our attention that certain clientele have been betting big and winning big. And, even though there are no issues with that, most of the folks we deal with up here, as you may already know, do not bet aggressively like these folks are," Sebastian explained.

"Would you like for me to cut them off?"

"Absolutely not, we just want to know who they are. Is there anything you can tell us about them?"

"It's two of them, and they're most certainly not from around here," Mickey explained.

"What do you mean by that?" Fabian asked as he returned back to his seat to resume counting money.

"Well, they're...well, don't take this the wrong way, but they're a lot like you guys. You know, from another city."

"You mean out-of-towners?" Sebastian asked.

"I don't mean any disrespect."

"None taken, I can assure you," Sebastian assured him.

"What are their names? What do they look like? What do they drink?"

"I've never paid attention to what they drink, because I'm dealing with other customers, but the guys I always deal with, one's name is Bobby, but I'm not too sure of the other guy's name he's with because he never talks," Mickey told them, noticing that he grabbed their full attention.

"Have they ever told you where they're from?" Khan immediately asked.

"No offense, but I'm not doing background checks on the spot when I'm dealing with people," he explained with a chuckle but stopped when he realized that they were not amused.

"You have a point there," Khan conceded. "Is there anything else?"

"Aside from their menacing demeanor, there is something I can't pinpoint when I'm dealing with them, which is often brief."

"Like what?" Frankie asked, curious.

"I don't know, but they seem close."

"What do you mean 'close'? Like bend for a friend close, or just two good friends close?"

"Again, I can't pinpoint it, but let's just say that I have a lot of friends, and I am by no means that close to any of them."

Khan and Fabian looked questioningly at each other, simultaneously wondering if the two men Fabian's partner, Angela, spoke to were indeed Avvi's hitmen. Khan, trying to recollect their names, caught the attention of everyone surrounding the table when he mumbled to himself, "Oh shit!"

"Alright Mickey, we appreciate what you've been doing for us, so do me a favor before you head back to work: the minute you see these guys, just let one of us know so that we can observe them, and observe them only," Sebastian requested, looking around at the rest of his crew.

"No problem," Mickey responded as he began to walk out of the office. Before leaving, he turned around to ask, "You wanted to know what they were drinking. Can I ask why?"

Sebastian, who smiled at his question, responded, "You can tell a lot about a person by what they drink."

"I'll keep that in mind," Mickey responded as he walked out.

"Is everything alright?" Sebastian asked Khan.

"I should have told you then, but when you left me here with the hog humper here a few weeks ago, Fabe and I saw these two guys sitting at the restaurant. They looked familiar, but I wasn't sure, so Fabian's colossal-size girlfriend spoke to them as if she was going to take their order. She explained to us that they were fags," Khan said.

"First of all, you're banging another barmaid that works here?" Sebastian asked.

"Yeah, you know who she is," Fabian replied.

"No, Fabe, we're too grossed out to look at your bitches, especially when they're laying out naked like sea lions basking in the sun. So, forgive us if we don't have the courage to pay attention to the monstrosity you like banging. Secondly," Sebastian turned to question Khan, "How the fuck could you overlook something as important as these two guys?"

"This Angela broad mentioned that they seemed like fags, so I left it alone."

"You left it alone? Why would you do that?"

"Because they were fags looking for martinis," Khan explained.

"Fuck me," Sebastian uttered out as he combed his hair with his fingers. "So, what now? Are you saying these two guys are Avvi's people? And they're both blowing each other?" Sebastian questioned

"I don't know, but this just got strange," Khan replied.

"Well, it's pretty obvious that these two guys don't know who's operating all of this. If they had, they would've tried to kill us or something, wouldn't you agree?" Khan asked.

"Maybe they're trying to muscle into uncharted territory by bankrupting local bookies and taking over," Fabian added.

"Or maybe they're two men looking for man-love in this establishment," Frankie jokingly said to them all.

"What the hell is going on in this world? Aren't there any real badass hitmen left in the world anymore? I tell you, the days of ruling with an iron fist have been replaced with booty beads and apple martinis," Fabian commented.

"What the hell did you just say? Booty beads? Really? I'm starting to worry about you, you half-a-fucking-fag, you," Sebastian fired back.

"No, I'm just saying that in today's world, compared to just twenty years ago, the men in this country have gotten soft. Men today are too in touch with the unsolvable emotions," Fabian replied.

"What the hell is wrong with you, using terms like unsolvable emotions? I don't even think that's a legitimate term, let alone an analogy," Sebastian said, tossing betting tickets up in the air out of frustration.

"No, I'm just saying that the world has gotten all liberalized, and everyone has been transformed into pussies," Fabian tried to justify his answer.

"No, I know what the hell you just said, and I can assure you that sort of shit is sick, Fabian."

"I'm not here to talk about cocktails or—"

"Careful how you say that word," Sebastian interrupted him, the whole office erupting into laughter.

"Hey, Mickey just called. Your two fag hitmen are in the lounge area, ready to collect their winnings," Frankie said to them, breaking up their argument.

"Listen up, I don't want anyone approaching them. Keep in mind where we're at," Sebastian told them as he slid back his pistol stop and placed it in his back holster.

He started delegating, "Khan, stay put. They know who you are, but they don't know us; at least, I don't think they do. Turd buglers or not, they'll eliminate you if they suspect that we're onto them." "Frankie, have a drink at the bar and keep your eye near the door. Fabian, stay near the back. Make sure they don't exit out that way and magically disappear." Sebastian grabbed his brother's arm and urged, "Fabe, I'm serious, don't become a hothead and get made out. We're still not in the clear."

"Fine."

"Adam, run to the apartment and get the money. Call me when you're on your way back."

"What are you going to do?" Frankie asked Sebastian as he opened the office door so that they could all exit out.

"I'm going to go to the kitchen, grab one of the cook's jackets and act like one of the Spanish waiters. I'll go from section to section, keeping my eye on Mickey."

"Gee, you really are going to get into character aren't you?"

"Screw you, Frankie."

* *

Like trained assassins, executing the element of invisibility, everyone took their places. Khan monitored the security camera feed in the office, his eyes glued to the menacing gay duo unwearyingly waiting for their payout.

Frankie, who undetectably made his way to the bar, recognized the one called Bobby from a collection that took place many years ago in Chicago. He identified him as none other than Robert Bianchi, a feared, freelance, for-hire hitman who worked for the Giordano crime family in Chicago.

"What the hell? Why is he here? Are they looking for us? After all, there is a price on our heads. Or is he trying to find a new home, free of any ridicule to his presumed lifestyle, while earning a living at the same time?" Frankie asked himself.

"Hello?" Sebastian answered Frankie's call.

"Sebastian, one of the maricones waiting for Mickey is Robert Bianchi," Frankie explained to him over the phone, from across the restaurant.

"Why does that name sound so familiar?"

"Avvi has used this guy to track deadbeats outside of Chicago."

"Shit, is that him?"

"I'm certain it is."

"So, what are you saying? Avvi's search team has found us?"

"I don't know, but if you think about it, if this guy was hired to find us and kill us, wouldn't he have done this a little differently? Like, take us out in a car, or in a more secluded area, free of witnesses?"

"You have a point there, but what is he doing here? I find it hard to believe that this is all a coincidence."

"I don't know, Sebastian. But these guys, homos or not, are no joke."

"Can you take him out, Frankie?"

"I can, I think. But, the other guy with him, I can't get a clear view of—"

"Oh shit," Frankie interjected. "That's Avvi's nephew, Ephraim."

"Are you sure?"

"He got a little on the heavy side, but yeah, that's him. You know, now that I think about it, that kid has always been light on his feet. Even Avvi realized it but never said anything because he was always a good earner. Frankie, what the hell do we do?"

"We need to regroup and analyze this because they haven't shown any threat to any of us. Any wrong move on our part can really affect all of us. Starting a war, or even getting arrested, is never a good thing."

"You're right. Call Fabian, tell him to stand down and the two of you come meet me upstairs. I'll go and meet up with Khan."

"Okay."

"Well, I guess you were right about your two hitmen," Sebastian said to Khan as he rushed into the office.

"I knew it," Khan replied.

"The one they call Bobby," Sebastian pointed on the security camera screen, "That's Robert Bianchi."

"Bianchi...Bianchi. Why does that name sound so familiar?" Khan questioned, trying to remember the name.

"Because he's the hitman for hire for the Giordano crime family."

"Sebastian, this isn't good."

"Yeah, no shit."

"What are we going to do?"

"I don't know, but I have that nervous, anxious feeling in the pit of my stomach."

"This is not good, Sebastian."

"Well, it doesn't end there. The guy with him is Ephraim," Sebastian said, pointing at the other man on camera.

"Okay, am I supposed to...NO! It can't be!" Khan yelled out in shock.

"Yes, it is."

"That's Avvi's nephew, Ephraim Lamski?" Khan asked as they turned away from the screen.

"Yup."

"He's a freaking passion fruit? What the hell is going on?" Khan asked as he and Sebastian walked over to the office bar to make a quick drink.

"Hold on, Frankie's calling me," Sebastian said. He answered the phone, "Hello…be right there," Hanging up, he said.

"Khan, we need to go. Our men of mystery downstairs have both Fabian and Mickey at gunpoint and are walking them, as we speak, behind the trash alley."

"Holy shit, this isn't good, Sebastian."

"Khan, you need to calm down. And whatever you do, do not shoot anyone unless your life or Fabian's life is in extreme danger. Do you understand me?" Sebastian asked Khan, who was in a deep state of shock.

"Khan!" he yelled out, snapping his brother out of his trance.

"I'm good, I just don't understand."

"Well, we need to be focused now, because this can potentially get really hostile," Sebastian explained as he placed an extra magazine in his pocket.

Taking a deep breath and mentally psyching themselves up to face the unknown, Khan and Sebastian looked at each other one last time, nodded in approval and exited out the back door that led them to the alleyway.

"I knew I recognized you," Ephraim Lamski told Fabian as he watched Khan and Sebastian enter the alley.

"No need for any of this to go the wrong way. Keep your hands crossed over your chest and walk slowly towards me,"

Bobby Bianchi directed them as he pointed his Silver Smith & Wesson SW1911 .45 ACP pistol their way.

"I really don't remember you much," Ephraim told Fabian. "But you, you I know. And my uncle will be happy when he finds out we've found you guys," he said to Khan with a victorious grin.

"Wait a minute, you're not here looking for us?" Sebastian asked.

"No. We're just looking for a new location to set up shop and go into business for ourselves. Is this place yours?" Ephraim asked.

"We made a couple of bucks here. So what's it to you?" Sebastian replied as he looked at Fabian, who was already measuring Ephraim.

"What's it to us? Well, if you must know, I will turn you over to the family, and once we are commended and rewarded, we will take over from here. But don't worry, my gentile friend, I will pick up and make better where you left off," Ephraim responded. He instructed Bobby Bianchi to keep an eye on them all while he made a phone call.

"So, this is the home to the Vikings?" Bobby Bianchi asked.

"Yup, their colors are appealing, don't you think?" Fabian sarcastically commented.

"What is that supposed to mean?"

"You know what it's supposed to mean."

"Fabian," Sebastian called out, hoping that he could stop his brother from further escalating their situation.

"No, fuck these fucking maricones! They are not going to come here and—" Fabian stopped his discriminative banter midsentence, frozen in disbelief as he listened to what he believed was Russian.

"Přijďte se se mnou setkat v zadní uličce. Tady je spousta lidí." (Come around and meet up with me in the back alley. There are a whole bunch of them here.) A burly, sonorous-voiced man spoke on his cell phone while pointing a gun at the back of Ephraim's head.

Fabian, who had never seen the Eastern European-looking man before, knew that he was not there to order the food from the restaurant, but was looking for the man that shot the Czech bodyguard at the Brooklyn Park apartment.

"I do not know what is going on here, but I can guarantee you all that none of you are walking out of here alive," the man shouted.

"Do we know you?" Khan nervously asked.

"Unless you want to be first killed, I would just be quiet, little Chinaman."

Khan, who always hated being called Chinese, could not help himself and replied, "I'm not Chinese, you Russian fuck. I'm Vietnamese."

"I am not Russian, I am Czechoslovakian."

"Really, what the fuck is the fucking difference?" Khan irately asked him.

"Well, fuck you then!" he yelled back in his Czech accent. He pointed his gun at Khan, causing him to turn his attention away from the others.

Fabian and Sebastian instinctively drew their guns and pointed them at the burly man who had dropped his guard.

"I don't think so, Evan Drago," Sebastian said. He and Fabian had clear shots. "I don't know what this is all about, but you are not shooting my brother."

"Shoot him!" Ephraim shouted at Fabian.

"Shut the fuck up, cock-taker. I couldn't care less about your faggot ass," Fabian angrily yelled, never losing sight of his Eastern European threat.

"This is the reason why this country is so screwed up," an aged, old-school capo-looking man addressed them all as he calmly presented himself in the midst of the all-guns-drawn confrontation.

"You want to embrace everyone and bypass personal prejudices. Trust me, it's always easier to live with yourself when your center of gravity is established," he continued explaining to the group as he lit up a cigarette.

"Who the hell are you?" Sebastian asked.

"Ask him," he replied, pointing to Fabian.

"Is this the guy?" Sebastian asked, never dropping his weapon.

"Yep," Fabian responded as he closed his dominant eye and began aligning his front sight at the new target's head.

"I would think twice about pulling that trigger if I were you," he warned Fabian.

"The same way you and Vladimir here determined that we should go as well? No thanks, I think it's you that needs to go so that we can finish up our business here."

"So, I guess you want a war, yes?"

"I didn't come uninvited; you did, my Czech intruder friend."

"Je to prase, které zabil mého bratra?" (Is this the pig that killed my brother?) the man who had his pistol pointed at Khan asked.

"Ne, ale je s nimi, takže je to stejně vinné." (No, but he is with them, so that makes him just as guilty.)

"English, you stupid commie fucks," Sebastian loudly said to them, showing signs of frustration.

"Tell you what, kid: if you shoot these Russian-looking fuckers, we can work something out," Bobby Bianchi told Fabian with a disingenuous look.

"Chystám ho zastřelit."(I am going to shoot him.)

"Ne." (No)

"Chystám ho zastřelit!" (I am going to shoot him!)

"Ne!" (No!) the Czech boss sternly ordered, avoiding gunfire for the moment.

"Tohle kurva zabil mého bratra a musí zemřít!" (This fuck killed my brother and he must die) the man yelled back as he felt the tension intensify within the circle.

"On cię nie zabił, bracie!" (He did not kill you brother, I did!) Adam shouted out in Polish to the man pointing a gun at Khan.

Frankie, who had quietly snuck up from behind, aimed his pistol and smiled at Khan, who showed signs of panic.

"Frankie, no!" Sebastian screamed out.

Bravado Brothers

✳ ✳

As he wiped off the sweet, metallic-smelling splatter that sprayed on his face and much of the front side of his body, Khan identified the distinctive sound of a .45 suppressor. His panic rose and the thump of multiple bodies hitting the ground changed the dynamics of their circumstance.

"You motherfuckers are going to pay for this! I'm going to make sure all of you will suffer a long and painful death!" Bobby Bianchi screamed out. He was watching his longtime friend and swinger partner lay lifeless on the ground in a pool of his own blood that was slowly making its way toward a storm drain. "You motherfuckers, I am going to kill you all," he continued yelling out as he began to weep. "You might as well kill me now, because—"

Bobby's eyes widened for the last time as a small fragment of his skull shot out from the back of his mouth and straight at Khan. Khan, who spit out the bone, followed by a stream of bile, began to clear his mouth.

"What the hell is wrong with you? You couldn't wait until I moved out of the way?" Khan screamed at Frankie. For the second time, he wiped away blood and brain splatter, this time from the head of Bobby Bianchi.

"Is it just me, or did any of you get tired of being threatened by this Guinea douchebag," Frankie said as he removed his suppressor and placed his pistol in its holster.

"This is really bad, Frankie."

"What the hell are you talking about, Fabian? We've seen worse in Iraq."

"No, Frankie, what I'm saying is that we just started a war with these fucking Czech folks, who we have no chance of winning against," Fabian said as he searched the inside of the Czechs' suit jackets.

"I don't know anything about them, but I can assure you that this Jew fuck here was going to turn us over to Heime. What the hell did you think was going to happen, Fabe?"

"We could have spoken to Avvi's nephew, whatever his name was, and convinced him that we had nothing to do with what happened to Avvi."

"Fabe, these two sissy hitmen were going to take over what we've built out here and turn it into a gay gambling operation."

"You don't know that, Frankie."

"Fabian, Frankie's right. They were going to turn us over, and you know that there would've been no compromising," Khan joined in as he removed his outer shirt and continued cleaning himself up.

"What about Red?" Fabian asked.

"What about him? It's not like he knows we're here," Frankie replied.

"Before you came and the two of you shot all these pricks, Ephraim left for a minute to make a call, more than likely to Chicago. Shortly after, these Czech fuckers showed up, and then you guys came into the picture," Sebastian explained as he looked around to see if there were any witnesses in the narrow alley.

"You mentioned Red. How do you know he called him and not someone else, like Heime?" Frankie asked.

"Frankie, it's the same shit. You know that Red was given the green light and he's coming for us," Sebastian said as he walked over to the bodies and began to drag them away from plain sight.

"Well, I guess there's no way of knowing. So, now what?" Frankie responded, helping Sebastian.

The sudden ringtone of traditional Irish bagpipes began to play from Ephraim's cell phone, freezing all five of them in place, no one uttering a word.

Khan, who was the closest person to Ephraim's body, shakily placed his hand inside Ephraim's pocket to remove the phone. "Shit, it must be on the other side," Khan commented to himself, immediately removing his hand.

"Well, shit, Khan, I just saw you grab something. Was it his cock or something?"

"Fuck you, Frankie. I'm the wrong motherfucker to fuck with. Do you understand me?" Khan aggressively challenged him.

"Someone pick up the phone, dammit," Sebastian shouted in frustration.

"I got it," Adam volunteered, breaking his unsettling silence. "There's no name on the caller ID, just a red circle where the picture should be, and it's a 312 area code," he explained to them in confusion.

Fabian realized that the red circle displayed on the phone was actually a symbol for Red. He placed his index finger over to lips to indicate that everyone should remain quiet, as he pressed to answer the call followed by the speaker button.

For several seconds, an eerie silence gripped everyone that circled around the call, immediately placing the five of them on edge. They knew that Avner's nephew, Ephraim, not answering revealed loud and clear to the caller that he wouldn't be answering any more calls.

Red's heavy breathing, which was distinctive to those who were close to him, transmitted a warning signal that Ephraim's departure was detrimental to anyone involved.

"I don't know who's listening, but I can assure you that there will be a price on your lives. That is, of course, if you reveal yourself," Red spoke.

Khan, who had worked with Red closely, knew that revealing any information was the equivalent of signing your own death sentence. He waved at his brothers and best friend to remain quiet.

"I hope this isn't who I think it is," Red commented before hanging up.

"Adam, destroy the phone. It's safe to say that this cell phone has a tracker on it," Sebastian ordered him.

"So, what are we going to do with these deep sleepers?" Adam asked as he noticed Sebastian's concerned look.

"I don't know, but we now have two major problems we're gonna have to deal with," Sebastian replied. "Shit's about to get real ugly."

Chapter XVII

Truth Is Like A Double Edge Sword

"So, let me get this straight. Ephraim left you a message about those assholes being in St. Paul, and now you can't get in touch with him?" Heime asked Red with an unsettling voice. "So, who answered the call if it wasn't him?"

"I don't know," Red replied, knowing that his answer was not acceptable.

"You've known these sons of bitches all your life, and you know what they're capable of. Do you think they got rid of him?" Heime asked as he stared out his window.

"Ephraim, I don't know, maybe; but Bobby, he's a badass, so the chance of that happening is unlikely," Red responded, sounding unsure.

"That is, of course, unless they got caught with their pants down, those fucking faygelehs," Heime replied, distaste in his voice.

"What do you mean?" Red questioned.

"Oh, stop it, you. Everyone knows that those two have been blowing each other for the longest time, so don't act like this is news, or I'll question your sincerity," Heime said to him.

"So now what?" Red asked with a smile.

"Now? Well, now I have to think about how this is going to get handled. But first, you're going to head up there, and hopefully confirm that Avvi's nephew is still alive."

"And if he isn't?"

"Red, just go up there and let me know, because right about now, I don't have a backup plan, should the news be bad. This is all not making any sense to me. Something just isn't right."

"Okay, I'll call you in a few days and let you know."

"Oh, one more thing Red: for now, keep this between us. Something tells me that this is all going to get ugly."

"Heime, if you were Avvi, you wouldn't appreciate not being told information like this."

"I know, Red. However, before you, I or whoever tells him, it needs to be considered that this sort of information requires facts, not speculations or assumptions."

"Heime, you know I didn't mean it that way."

"Red, if you were Jewish, I would have told you that you're a good Jewish boy for saying that."

"I just want to do this right, Heime."

"I know. You have a lot riding; not to mention, you'll now see how all the moving parts work, which is important if you're going to go your own way one day."

"Thank you."

"For what it's worth, I've always liked those Rodriguez boys. Not so much Franco, or whatever the hell you guys call him, but most certainly the three of them. Who knows, perhaps all of this can be straightened out," Heime said.

After several moments of silence. Heime told Red, "Go ahead kid, speak what's on your mind."

"Truth is like a double-edged sword. It will cut you one way or another," Red answered.

"We shall soon find out if the sword is battle-ready, my gentile brother. We shall soon find out."

Missing In Action

"What do you mean Mikolas cannot be found? Have you tried tracking his phone?" Mafia Pakhan (Boss) Hynek Červenka questioned one of his trusted henchmen, Josef Novotny.

"Yes, but there is no signal. Maybe he turned off his phone. You know how much he hates being tracked."

"He better not have. Where did he say he was going, again?" Hynek asked.

"He went to St. Paul to confirm the identity of the man who killed Andrej, his bodyguard."

"Why would he do that, and why didn't he tell me? He knows that we were going to get that Fena." (Son of a bitch)

"You know more than anyone that Mikolas will not listen to reason, only what he feels is right at that moment."

"Who are these people, anyway?" Hynek asked as he inspected his newly-arrived inventory of sex slaves from the Republic of Moldova.

"I am not too sure, all I know is that he believed they were Hispanic, possibly from Chicago, based on their accent and the way one of them dressed."

"So, now what? I have to wait for his call?"

"Hold on, boss, I need to pick up this call. It's from Mikolas' driver," Josef explained to Hynek. He went to the corner of the room to pick up the call

Born and raised in the brutal Hungaro-Slovak clan, and the primary architect of a multimillion-dollar American operation for over two decades, sixty-three-year-old Hynek Červenka was severely out of shape and suffered from various respiratory ailments. But he always sampled his new arrivals of seized young beauties from overseas; it was a perk he partook in that allowed him to stay connected with the old country, versus dealing with the spoiled rotten American girls he never found any pleasure in.

"Boss, are you alright?" Josef asked as he returned from his phone call. Hynek was panting and coughing after having his way with the delightful young girls who were ready to be marketed.

"Ano, ano," (Yes, yes.) Hynek, responded, putting his pants back on and lighting up a cigarette.

"That was Mikolas' driver. He is saying that it has been over forty-five minutes since he has seen him. He also mentioned that he went inside the restaurant, looking for Mikolas, and did not see him. Now Mikolas still has not come out. Something is not right, Hynek."

"I want you to go over there right away and see if you can find him," Hynek ordered him as he regained his breath.

"Consider it done."

"Listen to me, Josef. If anything has happened to him, do not do anything unless you have to. Once you return, we will assemble our punishing retaliation appropriately."

"Perhaps it's nothing," Josef replied.

"Let us hope you are right because another war would not be a good thing. Not to mention, the family from the Russian Bratva would not be too happy. They will view us as being weak, and that is not going to happen," Hynek explained in a solemn manner.

Sānt 'Pôl

"So, are you sure this is the location?" Josef Novotny asked Mikolas Jelinek's driver, Anton.

"Yes."

"And how long has it been now?"

"About ten hours."

"So, why haven't you gone inside?" Josef asked as he racked his pistol.

"I don't know about your boss, but when Mikolas says to stay in car, you stay in car," Anton replied, showing signs of apprehension.

"Well, I agree, my friend, but if Mikolas is not in the restaurant or is found dead, you are going to have to answer to Hynek," Josef explained as he stepped out of the car.

"Kretén," (Asshole) Anton commented to himself, watching Josef calmly walk toward the restaurant.

"Good day, sir, and welcome. Will it just be you today?" Khan greeted Josef, playing the role of a host.

Josef immediately scanned the restaurant and did not see anything out of the ordinary. He decided to sit quietly for reconnaissance. "I will take a seat for now at the bar. May I have a menu as well?" Josef requested with a smile.

"Of course, please follow me," Khan replied, showing him to an available seat at the bar.

"Anton, I need for you to go toward the back alleyway and see if you see anything. It's pretty busy in here, so I should be able to look around without being noticed," Josef directed over the phone.

"Yes, sir, boss," Anton replied as he racked his pistol and stepped out of his vehicle

"Anton."

"Yes?"

"Do not shoot anyone, do you understand me?"

"Chápu." (I understand.)

"Séf, Jsem v restuarantu," (Boss, I am in the restaurant) Josef notified Hynek over the phone.

"Dobrý. Jakmile potvrdíš, že Mikolas je naživu, zavolej mi ho." (Good. As soon as you confirm Mikolas is alive, have him call me.)

"Já budu." (I will)

"Josef."

"Ano, Séfe?" (Yes, boss?)

"Do not let Mikolas' driver anywhere near the restaurant. He is an idiot and will only get in the way."

Josef, who did not want to tell Hynek about the premature directives he gave to Anton just minutes ago, agreed with his superior. He immediately ended the phone call and ordered a vodka for a quick shot.

"Can you show me the bathroom?" Josef asked the bartender as he dialed Anton's number so that he could cancel his reconnaissance. "Shit," Josef mumbled, canceling the call that went to Anton's voicemail.

The door that led to the men's room was right beside the kitchen entrance. Josef observed the kitchen's ceaseless movement of personnel and grabbed a chef's coat from a hanger and a clipboard. Within the sea of white-dressed staff, Josef blended in as he made his way around, inspecting the kitchen, and finally arrived at the door leading to the cellar.

"This is why you should never freeze a body for so long. It doesn't help us when we need to be quick about things," Sebastian commented out of frustration.

"Well, if we don't do it this way, then there would be blood splattered everywhere, and you already know how Fabe reacts to the sight of blood," Frankie replied.

"Fuck you, Frankie, I've never had an issue with blood," Fabian confrontationally responded.

"I guess you're right. With you humping on those women the rest of the civilized world would consider cattle, you should be used to seeing disgusting things," Frankie shot back.

"Hey, Frankie, what do those Southern yahoos call it when a man has to prop up so they can hump on cattle?" Sebastian asked.

"Stump-broke," Frankie answered with a smile.

"Aren't you banging that new waitress?" Sebastian asked Fabian.

"Holy shit, you done stump-broke that new mule, already?" Frankie yelled out with a meager Southern accent.

Fabian, who was responsible for pushing the blood into a floor drain with a long-head rubber squeegee, stopped his actions. The disdain of his acquired taste for voluptuous women began to infuriate him.

"Let me tell you cocksuckers something—" Fabian started saying until he was interrupted by an unfamiliar voice.

"Why in this country do so many of the men call each other derogatory terms? For example, you just called him cocksucker?"

Sebastian, Frankie, and Fabian were all caught by surprise when they saw the unannounced guest got the drop on them, brandishing a large pistol. They all immediately wondered the whereabouts of Khan, who was supposed to be their lookout.

"Based on your silence, you are all thinking about cocks...Did I describe this incorrectly?" Josef questioned them.

He slowly walked toward a body covered with a plastic bag, on top of a table. "

"I only hope this is not who I think it is," Josef warned the three of them. The only noise made in response was the sound of his shoes detaching from the sticky, blood-stained floors.

"Kohoutky!" (Cocksuckers!) Josef yelled out in anger. Removing the bag from the body revealed Mikolas' henchman, lying lifeless on a stainless steel table used to slice steaks delivered to the restaurant.

"You, pretty man. You're first," Josef irately yelled at Fabian, pointing his pistol at his head, ready to squeeze the trigger.

"Tell me now, where is Mikolas!"

"I don't know who you are talking about, but there is no one here with that name," Sebastian nervously replied.

"I will give you to the count of three. If I do not see Mikolas, not only will you die on top of your poor craftsmanship, but I will make sure your whole family is annihilated," Josef threatened them all.

"I don't know who you are referring too, but you need to calm down and stop pointing that gun at us," Sebastian calmly told him.

"I warned you, you son bitch," Josef replied, displeased.

"You're not shooting anyone. And by the way, it's 'son-of-a-bitch'," Khan sternly told Josef as he stood behind him and pointed a pistol at his head.

"What the fuck, where have you been?" Fabian gratefully asked Khan.

"Sorry, Fabe, but I've been attending to customers wanting to have a seat in the restaurant."

Frankie, who was grateful that Khan came in the nick of time, began to laugh at the very idea of Khan attending to patrons, like a happy-to-see-you-china-man at a Chinese restaurant.

"Go ahead, you half-spic, half-pol motherfucker, and say a fucking Chinese joke about me. I dare you, motherfucker," Khan abruptly snapped in protest, eyeballing Frankie.

"Khan, chill the fuck out," Sebastian said, trying to calm him down. "You do have to admit, that shit is funny."

"Fuck you, too! Fuck all of you!" Khan yelled out to all of them, never losing focus on Josef.

"Zìjǐyīgèmáng, bùyàoqiāngguà," (Do yourself a favor, and don't get involved.) Josef said to Khan, showing he was familiar with the language.

"You motherfucker, are speaking to me in Chinese?" Khan furiously asked Josef, followed by the others howling with laughter.

Anton, who had undetectably walked in the restaurant's back entrance, peeked his head inside the cellar to inspect his surroundings. He immediately became enraged when he saw the bloody head of Mikolas' henchman sticking out at the edge of the table.

Retracting back to a dark corner to remain unnoticed, Anton listened to the muffled voices coming from the cellar and assumed that Josef had also been killed. Then, as he heard the laughter of several men, he glanced at the man in a white jacket, holding his arm up, ready to shoot.

"Všichni se to dostanou do hlavy," (They are all going to get it in the head) he whispered to himself, mentally preparing to enter the room blasting, avenging his comrades.

"What the hell?" Khan shouted out as he went down on one knee and frantically began to wipe his eyes and hack out the blood in his mouth.

Then, with a loud bang, clash, and thump, Sebastian, Fabian, and Frankie, who did not see any aggressive movement, stared at the floor, amazed when they saw the bodies of two men lying on the floor.

"That shit was close," Adam said to them as he inspected his kill and removed the suppressor from his pistol.

"I'm getting sick of this shit!" Khan angrily yelled, stomping off toward the bathroom to wash off his face, which was sprayed with blood.

"What the hell just happened?" Fabian asked, staring at the fresh pool of blood around the drain he had just squeegeed for several hours.

"I don't know, but this sucks," Sebastian replied.

"Ah, yeah, it does. We just added two more bodies that we now have to dispose of, not to mention the one in the freezer," Frankie counted.

"So, now what?" Fabian asked. He sat down and began to shake.

"Now? Well, now we'll be here for a real long time, chopping these Siberian bears up. I mean, look at these guys. Getting past their body hair alone will take hours," Sebastian replied as he shakenly lit up a cigarette.

"No, we won't. We're all going to go upstairs and have some drinks, and then I am going to call our friends in South St. Paul and have them take care of this mess of ours. This is fucked up, and it's only going to get worse from this point on," Khan told them, clearly upset, as he changed his shirt for the second time that day.

"Adam, I have to admit, we've spent some time fighting in the Gulf and have seen some shit out there, but not once have I ever seen anyone shoot two people with one bullet," Frankie said as he inspected the bodies and removed their personal belongings.

"Well, I didn't shoot twice, only once in the head of the big fucker laying on top of the other big fucker," Adam replied.

"What do you mean, you only shot once? Did it go through his head?" Sebastian questioned.

"No, I was walking the back alleyway and saw this big son of a bitch come through the back. When I saw him looking inside with his piece drawn, I immediately screwed on my silencer, went after him and shot him in the head. We must have both shot at the same time," Adam explained with a puzzled look on his face.

"Fuck, he's right. We all heard a shot and Adam silenced his gat," Fabian told them, rolling Anton over on his back, revealing his revolver.

"This is exactly what the fuck I am talking about," Khan told them as he began walking toward the stairs that led up to the restaurant. "This 'just getting lucky' shit is not happening for me anymore. I was doing well with Avvi, just being a voice. Now, I'm dodging bullets."

"Come on, Khan, stop being like that," Sebastian yelled out to him.

"No! I'm tired of dealing with you dumbasses. You can't do shit right, and when this is all over, I don't want to see your faces for a real long time," Khan fired back one last time before slamming the door.

"What the fuck is up his ass?" Frankie asked.

"That spit of shit he can never properly wipe off," Fabian responded, sending them all into hysterical laughter.

Chapter XVIII

Before Me, Was Once We.

"Son of a bitch. Sebastian has gotten fat," Red told Allen as he watched him cautiously walk out the restaurant.

"Well come on and let's get him."

"Al, I know you are tired, trust me, so am I, but you're not dealing with amateurs. Not to mention we don't know this neighborhood, and we don't know where the others are at; especially Frankie, who by the way will shoot you on site." Red explained.

"I am not afraid of that spic fuck."

"I am not saying that you are, but going in to take down one guy, and let me remind you that Sebastian is no slouch either, is not a good idea," Red replied displaying a dislike to Allen's remark.

"Whoa…whoa…whoa…Don't get all hostile with me Red. They're your friends, not mine."

"Let's get one thing straight Al. I am not here on a sympathy visit, nor am I going to sit here and have you tell me what I need to do—you understand me? Do you understand me?" Red sternly asked him.

"Yes."

"Before me, those men you want to rush up on, used to be considered as we. So if I have to get rid of them, it will be when I, and only I, confirm that they must go. I have a lot of history with them and until all this nonsense that took place at Avvi's, we were all one unit."

"Red, I meant no disrespect. I'm just really tired," Allen replied after staring at Red without saying a word for over ten seconds. "This has been a long and exhausting trip, and if I stay another day in this car I am going to lose it, man."

"Al, you are not the only one that is sick of sitting in a car for long period of time, but all of this needs to be done right; not to mention without being noticed."

"So what now?" Allen asked as he leaned his seat back.

"I guess for now we'll just wait, it's almost one in the morning and there is not a person in the street," replied Red as the very idea of not eating for well over nine hours psychologically begins to take its toll.

"What the hell is that?" Allen mumbled as the two remained motionless when they saw a small meat packing truck slowly park in front.

"Well that's just great, this asshole just had to park in front of the entrance," Allen commented lifting his seat back up. "Should I pull up a little?"

"No, they will hear the car turn on, not to mention they will see us move."

"Well not being able to view the entrance will drive me crazy," Allen explained as he tried to make out the shadowy faces.

"I know, but let's just hang tight...wait a minute, is that Frankie?"

"I can't see shit Red, where either going to have to walk out and take a closer look or drive around closer to get a better look," Allen explained him.

"Shit that's him," Red uttered out as he viewed Frankie turn the corner from the restaurant with a four-wheel warehouse hand truck, wheeling several large plastic bags covered in stretch wrap.

"Why aren't they doing all this moving from the back alleyway?" Allen whispered.

"I don't think that truck will fit in there. It's too narrow," Red replied with a puzzled look.

"What the hell are they doing?" Red questioned.

"I don't know but there is a car slowly cruising by behind us and it's not here to sightsee," Allen told Red, forcing the two to them to place their pistols between their legs ready to shoot.

"What the hell was that all about?" Allen asked as he watched a tinted out Mercedes slowly drive by.

"I don't know but something tells me that shit is about to get real ugly," Red responded.

"Shit there's another car creeping up. What the fuck you want to do Red?"

"Chill out Al. responding prematurely will not do us any good," Red replied as he remained still hoping he wouldn't get picked up.

"Red, I am not feeling good about this."

"Well, we can't drive away now."

"Well, we better do something soon because you two buddies Sebastian and Frankie just got in the back of the truck." Allen pointed out, "Do you recognize that driver?" Allen asked as he placed his hand on the ignition ready to turn on the car.

"No."

"Do you want to follow them?"

"Give it a couple of minutes, and then drive away."

"But what if we lose them?"

"Al, finding a meat truck driving at one in the morning will not be difficult to find, besides we don't know who the hell those two cars were or if they too were scoping out the premises."

"I hope you're right Red," Allen replied as he watched the truck make a U-turn and drive toward I-35.

"Go," Red ordered after watching the entrance for just over a minute.

With a casual pace, he watched from a distance as the truck's brake lights brightened from making a series of stops and turns. Allen, who was starting to white-knuckle as he firmly gripped the steering wheel, began to tunnel vision.

"Hey Al, you're alright?" Red asked, hoping to break his focus.

"Al!" he yelled out a second time, snapping him out of his trance.

"Sorry, Red."

"What the fuck man? You're starting to scare the shit out of me."

"I forgot to take my meds that's all," Allen said to him as he searches inside his pockets looking for his pill.

"What the hell do you mean you forgot to take your meds? What, for blood pressure or something?"

"No not really," he chuckled, "They're for my disorder."

"What the fuck is going on? What disorder?" Red asked with a concerned look.

"I thought you knew or at least Heime explained it to you."

"Okay, enough with all this shit, what disorder?"

"I am bipolar."

"Well, that just explains everything doesn't it."

"Sorry, Red, I thought it really didn't matter."

"What the fuck do you mean it wouldn't matter?"

"Well, I treat it, so it shouldn't affect you," Allen replied with a serious face.

"Let me ask you a question you crazy fuck. Before a person goes to the bathroom to take a really bad shit, wouldn't it be helpful in knowing that there is something to wipe their ass with?"

"I never thought about it that way," Allen replied as he thought about the legitimacy of his question.

"Is there anything else I should know about?"

"No," Allen replied as he thought about any issues worth sharing with him.

"I ask because I am placed in a position where I might have to potentially take out my childhood friends and truthfully, I don't know how I am going to respond if I have to do that, and no offense, but you are the last person I do not want to worry about because you forgetting to take your meds or whatever the fuck it is you're taking."

"Well don't worry about that Red; I will take care of them for you."

"Never mind Al, just keep driving."

"Where the hell are these jerk-offs heading to?" Red asked as he starting seeing signs for Harriet Island Regional Park.

"He just turned on Water Street, so kill the lights, Al."

"But it's dark and I can hardly see."

"Is driving in the dark another disorder you have?" Red annoyingly asked.

"What the fuck Red, I told you about my condition in confidence."

"Stop the fucking car and let me drive."

"No I'm fine, I will drive. I am just saying it's dark that's all."

"Look they just stopped at some boat company place," Red whispered. "Pull over."

With an overhead light dimly illuminating the boathouse sign, and the shadowy figures surreptitiously moving back and forth near the entrance leading to a docked ferry, Red and Allen, who stepped out of the vehicle, quietly walk behind the cover of trees, and remained silent as they tried to get a better view to the clandestine operation.

"Red I'm telling you something is not right,"

"So what are you saying, we should stop and leave this for another day?"

"No Red, what I am saying is that this is all too easy."

"There goes that huge plastic bag again," Red whispered

"Those are some fucking bodies," Allen commented with a cynical grin.

"Look, there a woman coming out of the ferry. Fuck she's got a rack on her."

"Really, Al? You're visually fucking her now? You don't even know if she looks good?"

"Red, since we have been out looking for your long lost buddies all this time, I haven't gotten my balls licked and I am all backed up."

"Al, I don't want to hear any more shit from you. You're starting to irk the shit out me with your conditions and everything else."

"I'm sorry, Red, it's just these meds gets my juices flowing and..."

"Shh...They're getting back in the truck. Let's get back in the car." Red interrupted him.

"Hey, Red, those are not your friends that got back in the truck."

"Are you sure?" Red asked as he tried to make out the men entering the truck.

"Yes. Those guys are guys are much smaller."

"What the fuck are we going to do now?"

"I don't know Red, but that ferry is casting off from the dock."

"Shit this is not good," Red angrily commented as he punched the dashboard.

"Look there is a posted schedule with a map of the ferry route," Red pointed out as he got out of the car to take a look.

"This Ferry route is not very long, so they are not going very far," He explained to Allen as he thought about what it was Sebastian and Frankie is up too.

"Should we follow the ferry?" Allen asked.

"No, that will be impossible; however, we should follow that truck. I bet you they are going too met up with them."

"But why? Why wouldn't they just drive those bodies all the way to their destination?" Allen asked as he turned on the car never losing eye contact with the truck.

"It makes sense if you think about it. If that truck gets pulled over, there wouldn't be any bodies inside the truck, which means they have the local police under their payroll in this jurisdiction, instead they transferred the bodies in the ferry to take them to another location."

"Shit, if your theory is correct, maybe those spic fucks are not as stupid after all."

"No Al, they are not. As a matter of fact, it makes sense. Go and follow that truck. If I am right, that truck will meet up with them."

Chapter XIX

Third Wheel

"I still don't understand why we couldn't run up on them when we had the chance. It was just the two of them behind a tree like lovers."

"This is the last time I am going to discuss this with you, Jardani. They were not behind a tree for intimate reasons, they were there watching someone."

"Perhaps you're right, Tawno. Perhaps they were there watching other men riding each other like farm animals.

Americans, especially the males, lack morality. It's the reason so many of them are never going to see Devel." (God)

"If they spot us because you are not keeping your distance, there will be consequences, Jardani."

"Yes, boss."

"Look, I understand that they disrespected your fiancé, Drina."

"Tawno, that fuck exposed her breast—in the freezer," he interrupted him. "That is more than a disrespect."

"I will not argue with you, and knowing who I am, I would have probably reacted the same way—especially with the set she has," Tawno bluntly told him. "But we must be patient and approach this with a clear head."

"Tawno—"

"I don't have time to explain anything to you right now, Jardani."

"Fine," Jardani replied. He continuously looked in his rearview mirror and noticed headlights from a distance.

"Where the hell are we?" Tawno asked.

"I believe this is South St. Paul."

"What the hell are these guys doing here?"

"I don't know, but wherever that truck is headed is where they will be."

"Are we near the river?" Tawno asked as he tried to identify the unusual odor that occupied the neighborhood.

"I believe so," Jardani responded. He pulled over and saw Red and Allen park several streets away from the truck they were following.

"Jardani, who is behind us? You have been eyeing someone for some time now."

"I don't know, but since we left that park, I have seen headlights never leaving my rearview."

"Cops?"

"I don't know, they turned off their lights when I parked. Should I continue driving and try to get rid of them?"

"Normally I would say yes, but look across the field. I believe the ferry that left the park is docking."

"Are you sure that's the same one? I can only see the top of the ferry," Jardini observed, opening his window to listen.

"I am not one-hundred percent sure, but if you think about it, the river leads this far down; not to mention, what boat of any kind at this time of night is out here ready to dock?"

"Look, the two man-lovers just stepped out of their car," Jardani commented, sliding his pistol hot.

"I am only going to say this once," Tawno said to him, pulling his arm back. "If you kill any of them, I will shoot you myself—do you understand?"

Tawno's stare of disapproval forced Jardani to refrain from protest. Instead, Jardani silently scowled at his boss's demand. The idea of allowing the man who humiliated his fiancé to walk away unscathed did not settle well with him.

"Jardani."

"Fine, Tawno, but when the time comes I want to kill him myself."

"When that time comes, and it will, he's all yours."

"What about the car behind us?" Jardani asked, taking one last look before exiting the car.

"If they are here for the same guys we are after, then perhaps that might be to our advantage."

"What if they are not?" Jardani asked as he took a swig from a flask.

"Then they have to go. You see, Jardani, perhaps you get to kill someone tonight after all."

"That fat, Irish prick-taig, however, is the one I want," Jardani expressed indignantly.

"What do you have in mind?" Tawno asked as the two furtively made their way toward the back of a closed meat processing warehouse.

"Well, it's been some time since we have organized a good ol' fashioned bare-knuckle fight. You know, the way our traveler ancestors did it for so many years."

"Jardani, our kind here in the states have turned into what one might consider civilized."

"What does that mean?"

"Although our people are and forever will be a force to be reckoned with, there are many better ways to make money or settle disputes. Do you understand?"

"Tawno, I hope—"

"Shh, get down," Tawno cut him off as the cranking sound of the warehouse's roll up gate forced them to crouch down. "

"Move over to the weeds," Tawno whispered.

"Shit, this is not good," Jardani said. He realized they both jumped into the saturated grassy area that was outside the warehouse."

"Out of all the areas surrounding this smelly cesspool that we could have jumped into for cover, we had to pick this one," he angrily whispered as the cold stagnant water soaked into his pants.

"Son of a bitch," Tawno muttered. Looking across the field, he saw both Red and Allen hiding behind a container flat car, watching the warehouse workers who were waiting for the ferry to stop near a makeshift floating dock.

"They are in our sights, let's just get them and drive them back to Superior," Jardani said as he moved to zero in on Allen, thinking about what he did to his fiancé.

"Patience, my friend. There's a lot happening right now and something tells me that these two idiots, whoever is in the car that was behind us, and the people in that ferry are all going to clash."

"How can you be so sure?" Jardani asked as the various sounds from the river and open grass field gabbed his attention.

"All the ingredients in this pot filled with shit are beginning to stew."

"Tawno, I hope you're right because this swamp grass really smells bad from the high tide and it is slowly creeping up my ass."

"And you call those two over there man lovers?" Tawno replied, grossed out by Jardani's statement.

Bravado Brothers

✳ ✳

"I hope these guys are legit," Sebastian said to Frankie. They were watching a small group of Asian men and women in rubberized aprons and knee-high rubber boots make their way to the floating dock, patiently waiting for the ferry.

"How the fuck does he do it? I mean, he can't even speak their fucking language, that Viet Cong-gook motherfucker," Frankie said as he skeptically stared at the workers who were impassively staring back at them. "I don't even think they're Vietnamese."

"What the hell are they then?" Sebastian asked.

"I don't fucking know. All I know is that Khan was raised Puerto Rican, and if these folks ever find out that he isn't one of them, shit can get real ugly."

"What the fuck does that mean, 'he's not one of them'?"

"Sebastian, Khan speaks Spanish, about ninety percent of his diet is of Puerto Rican cuisine, and his mannerisms are that of a Latin man…he even gets down on playing a little cuatro (Puerto Rican Guitar) in parrandas (Christmas festivities). I mean, what the fuck?"

With a slight chuckle as he reflected on all the events that Khan so loved and enjoyed, especially during the Christmas holidays, Sebastian glanced around the darkened perimeter and nonchalantly commented, "My mother loves him. Loves him the way a mother loves her own child."

"How the fuck did we end up knee-deep in this shit anyway?" Frankie randomly asked.

"I don't know, Frankie, but somehow, someway, we have to get out of this mess. And Khan, regardless of who he is, has managed to work this out for us. So, let's get this done and over with and attend to bigger things, like Sean."

"Oh yeah, I forgot about that Mic-fuck," Frankie replied as he tossed the ferry line at the makeshift dock. "Do you really believe we're going to have to go to war with our best friend?"

"I hope not," Sebastian said. The thought of going to war stressed him out.

"Sebastian, these fucking Russians, or whatever the hell they are, are heavy."

"We'll just drag them out onto the deck and let the Asians do all the lifting. I believe these folks are being paid well," Sebastian told him, watching them walk up the foot plank.

"Đã được Khan?" (Where is Khan?) a female worker asked.

"I don't understand what you are saying," Frankie replied to her.

"Đã được Khan?" (Where is Khan?)

"Sebastian, what the hell is she saying?"

"Really, are you serious, Frankie? You're asking me what the hell she's asking?"

"I don't understand what you're saying," Frankie tried to explain.

"She say Khan no here, deal off," a young Vietnamese man spoke up.

"He will be here soon, I can assure you," Sebastian told him.

"Then you tell Khan to call," he replied back and motioned all the workers to turn around and exit the ferry.

"No, no, no, don't go! I am sure he is coming any minute," Sebastian disquietly assured him as he watched the warehouse workers nervously leave one by one.

"What the fuck are we going to do? Adam's big-titi'd ship captain girlfriend is starting to nervously look out the window," Frankie said to Sabastian as he began frustratedly dragging the bodies back in the cabin.

"What the fuck did you tell them?" Fabian yelled out as he ran up the foot plank and approached Sebastian and Frankie.

"We didn't say anything to these rice patty niggers, they left on their own because Khan wasn't here. Speaking of which, where is he?" Sebastian asked as he sat down to rest, exhaustion starting to take a toll on his body.

"At the moment he's talking to his contact over the speakerphone with the workers," Fabian answered. His anxiety began to heighten when he looked at the plastic wrapped corpses.

"I don't understand why they couldn't just take these bags from us when they first got here," Frankie said.

"Because we're not their people," Fabian said as he received the signal from Khan to prepare for the workers to board.

"Neither is Khan," Sebastian argued, helping Frankie drag the bodies back out onto the deck.

"What, you think we would have been able to pull this off with the resources we have out here? Maybe in Chi-Town we could have made some calls and gotten it handled, but out here," said Fabian as he walked to help both Frankie and Sebastian, who were both struggling with the bodies, "I don't think so."

"Oh shit, what the fuck is going on here?" Sebastian blurted out as he dropped the body and pulled out his pistol. He, Frankie and Fabian helplessly watched Khan and the warehouse workers walk up the narrow plank and onto the Ferry deck with their hands up in the air.

"Please, there is no need to make this an ugly situation," a corpulent Eastern European man said to them.

"Something we can help you with?" Sebastian asked.

"Please, you pointing the gun at me makes me nervous. Besides, a lot of dead Chinamen on a pretty-looking vessel like this is going to require a lot of cleaning up and a lot of explaining," the man replied.

"I don't know what it is you are looking for, but this is a private charter," Sebastian explained as he lowered his pistol. He stared at the two massive men who accompanied the man speaking to him.

With a thunderous laughter that was sardonic in tone, the man standing between the two Eastern European men looked at the two large bags lying on deck then turned toward Sebastian, trying to read his cloaked facial expression.

"So, what's in the bag?" he asked Sebastian as he pulled out a pack of cigarettes and lit one up.

Sebastian figured from their distinguishable Eastern European appearance that these three men were there to find their friends. Having already taken their friends out at the restaurant, he decided to remain silent.

"So, you don't want to talk?" he asked Sebastian. "Okay."

"Zastřelte jednu z těchto špiček v hlavě a leštiny vidí, jestli to upoutá jejich pozornost." (Shoot one of these chinks in the head and let's see if that grabs their attention.)

There was a blast that caught all those who were held captive by surprise, but Sebastian, Frankie, and Fabian all remained unfazed by the flash that lit up their faces. However, the splash from a Vietnamese worker falling in the water after being shot in the head made them start to realize what should have been a simple disposal and return back the restaurant before sunrise was now becoming an anxiety-inducing situation.

"Opravdu? Museli jste udělat všechen ten hluk?" (Really? You had to make all that noise?)

"Omlouvám se nad bossem," (Sorry, boss) one of the bodyguards said, immediately attaching his suppresser onto his pistol and shooting another worker in the head, sending him plummeting into the river.

"My apologies for the noise. I can assure you that he did not mean to disturb any of the resting wildlife in the area or disrupt the surrounding ecosystem here, but he is, what one would say in this country, rough around the edges," the man explained with a merciless smile.

"That's some sick shit, I have to admit. Not even I would have pulled that off with a straight face," Frankie said as he slightly bent over to see if he could locate a body floating in the river's murky water.

"Can you please do me a favor and tell these trifling species of people to remain quiet," the man requested to Sebastian. The weeping from the remaining warehouse coworkers began to annoy him.

"I don't speak their language," Sebastian replied.

"You know, I did not consider that and perhaps you are right," he said with a smile, and he visually gave the okay to his henchmen to start killing off the workers one by one.

Khan stood the closest to the henchmen and would be the first one to be killed off. He looked at his brothers with fear, as the possibility that he would escape his dire situation became nearly impossible.

"Me, personally, I couldn't care less about some migrant warehouse workers you feel are a threat to you, so go ahead and kill them off. But I can assure you that when it comes to us, it will be your last order, whoever the fuck you are," Sebastian threatened as he aimed his gun at the boss' head.

"Ne!" (No!) he immediately ordered his bodyguards, who were ready start shooting at Sebastian and anyone standing in their way.

"I don't know who the fuck you guys are, but I'm starting to lose my patience," said Frankie, displaying a readiness to shoot.

"Where are my manners? I am Hynek Červenka, and who I am should be of great concern to you."

"Now, I will say that name—which, by the way, sounds very threatening—is not familiar to me. But, since I now know who you are, I have a second question for you Mr. Hynek: Why are you here? What is it you want from us?" asked Sebastian.

"So, you get to know my name, but I cannot know yours? That is pretty disrespectful," Hynek reprimanded with a staid face.

"Sebastian."

"Well, Mr. Sebastian, why don't we all place our guns down and let's talk like civilized businessmen?"

"Talk about what?" Fabian asked.

"Okay, I see you guys are not going to cooperate and it's starting to piss me off, so let's cut the bullshit. What's in the bag?" Hynek asked, never losing eye contact with Sebastian.

"Our dirty laundry, and these men you want to get rid of are our personal dry cleaning service. What the fuck is it to you?" Sebastian demanded.

With a raspy laughter, followed by a wheezing cough that disoriented him, Hynek held onto one of his henchmen, pulled out a pack of smokes for the second time during their conversation, placed a cigarette on his lips and lit up.

"I have been living in this country for well over thirty years and I am still to this day amused by people in our business and their analogies," Hynek addressed the three of them as he straightened himself.

"People in our business? What do you mean 'people in our business'?" Sebastian asked.

"I don't have time for bullshit my Mexican friend—"

"Mexican?" Fabian snapped back. "Who the fuck are you calling Mexican? We're Puerto Rican."

"Speak for yourself, Fabian," Frankie interjected.

"Same shit, different toilet bowl," Hynek said with an apathetic demeanor. "I came all the way to this shithole for one reason and one reason only, so let's cut the shit out and open the fucking bag."

"I tell you what, my Russian friend—you fucking do it."

"Touché, my friend. Although we are not Russian, I appreciate your retort," Hynek replied with a smile.

"Otevřete tašku," (Open the bag) he ordered one of his henchmen.

"Hynek, Nevěřím těmhle divočím," (I don't trust these savages) his henchman said with a disdainful look at Sebastian.

"Jen to otevřete. Jestli je to Mikolas, zabijeme je všechny," (Just open it. If it is Mikolas, we will kill them all) Hynek said, never losing eye contact with Sebastian.

"Get the fuck out," Hynek's henchman yelled at Fabian, who was standing over one of the bags.

"No problem, pendejo," (Stupid) Fabian replied with a smile. He watched the henchman place his large caliber pistol inside his shoulder holster and remove a karambit folding knife from his waist. Fabian turned to Frankie and muttered,

"Este es el primero hijo de puta que voy a disparar." (This is the first motherfucker I will shoot.)

Grabbing the body bag from the head and forcing the body to sit up, Hynek's henchman began to slice open the bag below the neckline. He was angered when the foul-smelling blood started pouring out and streaming down his hand and wrist.

"Tito hloupí idiotové nikdy správně nevyčerpali krev," (These stupid idiots never properly drained the blood.) he said, wincing as the stench of the blood and flesh began to saturate the air.

"Hey, Fabe, this is what it smells like in your room when you bang those behemoth animals you call women."

"Fuck you, Frankie!"

"The two of you shut the fuck up!" Sebastian sternly said to them.

"Tam je amatér, co jste čekal?" (They're amateurs, what did you expect?) Hynek asked. He removed a handkerchief from his pocket and placed it over his nose and mouth as he looked in displeasure at both Fabian and Frankie.

"Jděte dál a vyjměte tašku tak, abychom viděli obličej," (Go on and remove the bag so that we can see the face.) Hynek ordered.

"To není on," (It's not him.) said his henchman as he looked at the pale face of a man he had never seen before.

"The next one," commanded Hynek.

"You forget to drain blood," Hynek's henchman said to Fabian. He dropped the stiffening body, stepped on its stomach and moved onto the next wrapped body.

Frankie showed no signs of being intimidated by Hynek's menacing bodyguard. He returned a sneering smile as he unwaveringly stood in front of him and watched as the bodyguard bent down and forcefully sat the body up that was showing signs of rigor mortis.

"Není to on nebo řidič," (It's not him or the driver.) he confirmed to Hynek as he slit the bag open and removed the plastic off the face.

"I am not going to even waste my time and argue with you about my comrade visiting the restaurant, but I know that all of you know where he can be found. I don't know how, but you all know," Hynek explained, frustration starting to exhaust his patience.

"What did he look like?" Fabian sarcastically asked.

"I tell you what," said Hynek as he removed his cell phone from his waist clip. "I will call one more time, and if I don't hear from him, a lot of us will not see the sunrise."

"Prosím neberte," (Please don't pick up) Hynek's second bodyguard uttered. He wanted so desperately to get into a shootout with the three men whom he felt were unworthy of their way of life.

A muffled ringtone sounded off the theme song from The Godfather—it was a ringtone that had amusingly been assigned to Hynek's number on his longtime friend and brigadier to his Bratva's cell phone. The noise coming from Mikolas Jelinek's phone caught their attention, and all three of them stopped moving in order locate where it was coming from.

The ringtone, which sent quivers down the spines of Sebastian, Fabian, and Frankie, forced them to look at Hynek, who was staring at one of the bodies and slowly shaking his head in disbelief.

"Odkud to pochází?" (Where is that coming from?) Hynek asked, looking around to locate its source.

"Od jednoho těla." (From one of the bodies.)

Sebastian glanced at his younger brother, Fabian, who was assigned to clearing out and destroying personal items from all the bodies. He visually questioned him as the ringtone continued sounding off.

"Ukončete hovor a opakujte volání pouze pro potvrzení," (End the call and redial just to confirm) one of Hynek's bodyguards suggested.

Hynek, who did not want to believe what he was listening to, ended the call and redialed as suggested. As clear as the night, *The Godfather* theme song ringtone sounded off again from one of the bodies.

Hynek furiously stared at Sebastian and snapped his fingers to his bodyguard.

* *

"What the hell is that?"

"What, are you serious?" Allen asked him.

"Why the fuck do you think I am asking you?"

"It's a spyglass monocular."

"It's a what?"

"A spyglass monocular."

"You said that already…what the hell are you going to use that for?"

"Red, how can you be in this line of work for so long and not be prepared for a little recon," Allen whispered.

"Let me see that shit."

"It's pretty cool, right?"

"Why didn't you pull this out when we were at the park watching them enter the ferry?"

"Because we were close enough to see clearly."

"Al, I feel like a fucking pirate with this thing; besides, I can't see shit. Here, you do the recon and tell me what's going on."

"Well, no wonder you can't see anything—you didn't turn on the night vision."

Annoyed and frustrated by Allen's know-it-all commentaries, Red turned his attention toward the ferry to try and make out the shadowy figures occupying its deck.

"It's too damn dark out here. Maybe if we move closer we can get a better view of what's happening," Red suggested. He looked around his surroundings one last time to make sure his immediate area was clear of hostiles.

Allen, who scoped his own immediate area, grabbed Red's arm and pointed about fifty yards across the field where Tawno and Jardani were lying on the marshy ground, observing the activity taking place on the ferry.

"Is that who I think it is?" Red asked in confusion.

"It sure is. So what do you want to do now?" Allen asked, looking around again and scanning their surroundings for any potential threats.

"Well, we just can't go in and start busting shit up on the ferry with these chuck wagon traveling nomads laying out on the field, doing whatever the fuck it is that they're doing," said Red as he started wiping his pants to remove the bugs. "But we have to do something fast because lying out here in the dark with God-knows-what crawling up our asses is freaking me the fuck out."

"Well, the only option for us is to go and meet up with these gypsy kings and get rid of them once and for all," said Allen as he placed his spyglass in his pocket and screwed the suppressor on his pistol

"Al, please, whatever you do, do not start blasting away just because you want to get rid of a problem. Let me speak with them—"

"And speak to them about what, Red?" Allen whispered. "Forming a truce? Fuck them. We're here to get your friends back home so that they can be dealt with and answer to their fuck-ups, whether they were responsible or not; and if that can't be accomplished, we're here to have them killed. I'm sure that will suffice for my employer."

Red, who was not content with Allen's reply, had forgotten why they were out in the middle of nowhere looking for his friends. He knew deep inside, one way or another, that justice was a hard pill to swallow.

"Look, Red," Allen said under his breath, breaking Red's deliberation, "I mean no disrespect, you know this, and I meant what I said about joining you one day when you are on your own, but right now at this very moment, I'm tired, I'm a stranger in a strange land, and I was hired by your boss, not hired by you. So, what happens here today is only business. I'm sure if it were you who had hired me to do this job, you wouldn't have wanted me to take any of this personally because, in the end, it's all business."

With a consenting gaze that exhibited indebtedness and respect, Red scoped his surroundings, pulled out a dull black suppressor, screwed it on his pistol, and took a deep breath to extract what little energy he has left in his fatigued body.

"Let's do this," Red said to Allen, who also showed signs of enervation.

Realizing the cool, moonlit sky was just hours away from dawn, which would remove all element of surprise, Red and Allen managed to undetectably cross over a set of train tracks that led them back to a dimly lit street. They cautiously reentered the soiled grasslands directly behind them and slowly walked toward their two targets, patiently waiting for their moment to strike

"Something doesn't seem right, Al," whispered Red.

"What do you mean?"

"I mean look at them, they're not moving."

"Maybe they're sleeping. They've also been up for a real long time looking for us," Al replied as he yawned and looked at his watch.

"Nah, something just isn't right. It's almost as if they're stuck or something," Red observed as he pulled back his slide to confirm he had a bullet in the chamber.

"Well, I don't know about you, but these fuckers have got to go," Allen said. He placed on black leather gloves and expanded a garrote wire.

"Al, really? Did you get that from the same place you got that pirate's scope or whatever it is you call that thing?"

"Well, as a matter of fact, I did. However, it's called a—"

"What the fuck was that?" Red hissed as he crouched down for cover. "It sounded like a gunshot and water splashing."

"That was more than water splashing—that was a splash from a body being shot and tossed over the ferry," Allen responded while he tactically laid on the wet grasslands and pulled out his monocular to view the ferry's deck.

"Fuck," Red mumbled in frustration, covering his face with the palm of his hand. "It's just the two of us out here in this swampy, bug-infested shithole, and I'm missing my Rem 700…What the fuck was that?" Red asked as a second splash from the river caught his attention.

"I wish not to impede on your unremitting surge of grievance you have chosen me to be part of, however, if I am viewing this correctly, another body just fell from the ferry," Allen conveyed.

"Are you serious? But there was no gunshot," Red said, readying himself for the unexpected.

"You're right. Of course, that muzzle was silenced," Allen told him.

"This is not fucking good, Al."

"What would you like to do?" Allen asked with a devilish smile.

"Well, these two camper smuggling humps need to be removed from the equation, and whether we want to or not, we somehow, someway are gonna have to get on that boat."

"To do fucking what, Red?"

"I'm not gonna let them go out like that! I…I mean we need to find out the truth before we start ending lives here."

"You know what, Red? I'm not even going to argue with you about your friends," Allen said as he put his monocular away.

Committed to removing the gypsies from the situation, Red pointed at Tawno, who was laying facing the ferry. Red's body started to tremble from lack of sleep and food as he began to slowly walk towards Tawno and Jardani, his footsteps masked by the river's calm burble.

"Why aren't these guys moving?" Red thought to himself when he heard the faint voice of Tawno talking.

"We're at South St. Paul off of Hardman Avenue. I will leave my phone on so that you can pick up our location—"

"I don't think so," Red yelled out from behind Tawno and removed the phone from his hands, stopping him from revealing more information to his people.

Tawno was caught by surprise and stuck from the river's sediment overflow that blanketed the marsh-like grassy plains. Now cold, exhausted and psychologically defeated, he watched his newly-formed nemesis grab his only functioning source of communication and toss it into the river the way a person tosses a flat stone so that it skips across the surface.

"You narrow back, bogtrotter, green nigger motherfucker. I promise you, you are going to pay for this. Your children, family, and everyone you love will—"

"I never thought that fat fortune-telling fuck would ever shut the fuck up," Allen angrily whispered as he bent down on one knee, breathing deeply from wrestling Jardani and repeatedly kicking Tawno unconscious.

"Al, are you serious? You zip tied this fuck over the mouth like a bridle on a horse?"

"I couldn't just have him yell or threaten us with all this nonsense happening, so yeah, I zip tied the fucker. One less thing we have to worry about," Allen replied as he admired his handiwork done on Jardani.

"Fuck," Red uttered out. As he looked around, he saw a lot of movement happening on the ferry.

"What's wrong, Red?"

"When I was a kid, I used to sense when bad shit was about to happen—this certain odor would grab my attention. I used to call it the smell of death."

"So, are you smelling this now?"

"Yeah, I guess," Red confirmed as he focused his attention on all the activity taking place on the ferry.

"Well, I don't know about you, but this whole area smells like shit, Red. Not to mention, we're near a meat processing plant—maybe that's what you're smelling."

"Take out that pirate scope and look at the deck; there's a lot going on," Red told Allen, squatting down and positioning himself near the ferry.

"Oh, shit, some big fucking Russian bear-looking guy is slicing a bag open. Fuck, a head just slid out of it," Allen relayed to Red as he immediately zoomed in on the ferry with his monocular.

"What do you mean it slid out, like it fell?"

"No, but I can definitely see a bloody face," Allen replied, trying to focus on the face.

"Is it Ephraim's or Bobby's?"

"I can't see it clearly, but this shit just got real ugly, Red. I mean, what the fuck did your buddies get into?" Allen commented as he began scoping across the ferry.

"What do you mean?"

"What I mean is what should have been a simple find and return looks like it will be a full-scale F.B.I. investigation."

"Well, no one is going to find out."

"If you say so, Red."

"What the fuck does that mean?"

"What it means is that there is a ferry, operated by the city, out in the middle of nowhere, docked in an area not designated for a vessel of its capacity, with dead motherfuckers on board and Chinamen huddled around. I don't know about you, but all this shit screams out crime scene."

Red, who was too tired to respond to Allen's veracity, could only bow his head in exhaustion, pull out his pistol, and forcefully generate every ounce of resolve he had left to move forward in entering the boat by surprise.

"Wait a minute, I see that Asian friend of yours. At least, I think that's him—I mean, there are a bunch of other chinks with him."

"What about the others—Sebastian or Frankie?" Red asked with an anxious look.

"There are too many of those lifebuoys around the rails, it's too hard for me to see anything clearly."

"Shit, this is all driving me crazy," Red snapped in frustration as the once-placid silent night began to take its toll on his body.

"Oh shit, there are guns drawn out everywhere," Allen unexpectedly muttered.

Then, a loud shot that pierced the silence of the night seized the dynamics of their situation.

Chapter XX

By Virtue Of

"I will no longer stand here and be disrespected by pretend gangsters. I gave you the opportunity to be honest and you all chose to die instead. So be it," Hynek scornfully said to them with a curmudgeon stare.

"Zabít je všechny!" (Kill them all!) he ordered his henchmen.

"Wait!" Khan yelled out, halting the gunfire. "What is it that you want?"

"Mluvčí mluví anglicky," (The stowaway speaks English) Hynek's bodyguard commented as he turned to look at his cohort with a sinister grin.

"Fuck him, and let's get this over with," the second bodyguard replied in a mild Eastern European accent, before lifting up his pistol and randomly aiming at the group of Vietnamese workers.

* *

The early morning waning moonlight exposed the fear and trepidation in the captives' silhouetted eyes as they unwillingly huddled around the ferry's deck. A blinding flash, resembling a bolt of lightning, ceased all movement for several seconds, and Sebastian, Fabian, Frankie and the hired clean-up crew remained mesmerized in disbelief by the action that unfolded.

The horrifying reality disabled everyone's reactionary abilities, and they were unable to shield themselves from the warm, unforeseen splatter that sprayed across their faces. The loud, cracking gunshots echoing across the cool morning air revealed to them all that death was among them and rearing its ugly head.

Khan, who received the brunt of the projectile assault, dropped down to a knee and, without warning, found himself landing face first on the deck. He immediately began to panic as the muffled screams and frantic pandemonium prohibited him from standing.

"Khan, are you alright?" Fabian shouted out, removing him from the skirmish path.

"What the fuck?" Khan yelled, cleared his eyes and spitting out small pieces of bone fragment once more. "I hope and pray none of these fucks have any incurable diseases."

"Shit, Khan, you're right, I don't know what I—"

"Shut the fuck up, you stupid fuck. This is all your fault for not getting rid of the phones," Khan irately raved at Fabian, his eyes glancing over at one of Hynek's bodyguards laying on the ground with a bullet through his eye socket.

"No, no, no, no!" Sebastian yelled, trying to stop the stampede of angry Asian workers rushing toward Hynek's second bodyguard.

The second bodyguard, who had just pushed Hynek over the rails, sending him plummeting into the murky and cold river, turned around to face the incensed Asian workers. The mob was aggressively moving in to attack, when the bodyguard pointed his gun at them and began shooting anyone crossing his path.

Many of the workers were formally trained in Vovinam practices and swayed their bodies to avoid their demise. As if spiritually channeling ancient warrior monks ready to combat their oppressors, the workers stabbed and bludgeoned Hynek's henchman, leaving him screaming in pain as the manifold of piercing blades severed his connection with life.

Frankie, who was amused by the savagery unfolding before his eyes, directed his attention at his best friends, who stared at the massacre in disbelief. He smiled at their grimacing faces when they turned away from the gore.

"Look up," Frankie said in a sotto voice, pointing up at the bridge where Adam was. He had shot the first bodyguard, getting them out of their quandary.

Adam shone a high-powered flashlight at the water and spotted Hynek trying to get to dry ground. He pointed his rifle at the Mafia boss, ready to stop him in case he decided to make a run for it.

"What the fuck just happened?" Khan angrily screamed, wiping the blood from his face.

"What the fuck happened to you?" Fabian innocently asked.

"You son of a bitch," Khan irately shouted back, and he lunged at Fabian, grabbing his shoulder and neck.

"Calm the hell down," Sebastian yelled, pulling Khan away from Fabian. "

"When this is over, you can beat the shit out of him all you want, but for now, we all have to exit this fucking crime scene boat here and fish that Russian fuck from the water; who, by the way, will prove to be a serious fucking problem."

Sebastian, Khan and the rest of their crew all looked overboard and watched Hynek slowly get out of the river and bend down on one knee, breathing heavily on land.

"Khan, this here is not good for any of us. We are tired, hungry and a lot of people have died today—it's overwhelming. So, do me a favor and go over to them and explain to these ginzu-slicing fuckers to get rid of the bodies right away. And please have them clean this boat up, it needs to go back into public service in just a few hours. I will see you shortly and please be careful, this isn't over yet," Sebastian calmly asked of him as he looked around the ferry, disgusted with its condition.

"Fine, but you keep that mammoth-humping son of a bitch away from me," Khan replied to Sebastian as he stared down Fabian, who was smirking directly at him.

"What are we going to do with that fat slab of shit?" Frankie asked while looking over at Hynek trying to walk on the unstable terrain with one shoe.

"I don't know, but I have this eerie feeling that we're not alone out here," Sebastian said. "And make no mistake, this night is far from over."

Sebastian lit up a cigarette and began walking toward the foot-plank in order to impede Hynek's escape.

"I promise you that all of you will suffer a long painful death," Hynek said to Sebastian, Fabian, and Frankie as they met up with him on the shoreline.

"I don't know who you are—and believe me when I tell you that I couldn't give a rat's ass when it comes to who you are—but you're going to have to come with us," Frankie ordered him.

"The only way I am going anywhere with anyone is if you shoot me and carry me dead," Hynek angrily replied.

"Well, today is your lucky day because I am in a good fucking mood, you fat blob of shit," Frankie sputtered out as he pulled out his pistol and aimed at Hynek's head. "So, if that's what you want, you got it."

"No," Sebastian yelled at Frankie. He wrestled his friend to the ground with the help of Fabian, who immediately stopped when the sound of a gunshot echoed across the field.

"What the fuck are you doing?" Sebastian asked Frankie, whose heartbeat was pounding through his layer of clothing.

"Well, the fat fuck wanted to be taken out, so I was gonna take him out."

"Ahh, Sabastian, we might have a small situation here," Fabian said with concern.

"Calm the fuck down," Sebastian warned Frankie for the last time. He turned his attention toward his younger brother who was standing in amazement and looked between him and Hynek laying on the ground. He asked Frankie, "What the fuck, I thought you shot into the air?"

"No, you two douchebags didn't let me get a shot out," Frankie shouted, aggressively grabbing his pistol from Sebastian's hand.

"What the fuck do you mean you didn't get a shot out? Look at him, he's lying on the ground bleeding," Sebastian pointed out to Frankie.

"That's because I shot that fat fuck myself," a familiar voice said to them.

Sebastian, Fabian, and Frankie remained motionless for several seconds as they stared at two silhouetted figures walk toward them. They remained in disbelief as the unsettling moonlight revealed the faces they had been running away from for some time.

"Aaaayy, looks who's here," Frankie sarcastically greeted Red while staring at Allen, who challengingly stared back.

"What's up, Sebastian? It's been a long time," Red greeted him.

"Not long enough."

"What does that mean?"

"You know what it means," said Sebastian, observing Red and Allen's every move.

"If I were you, I would chill the fuck out. This doesn't need to get ugly," Red warned Fabian as he watched him prepare himself to shoot.

"From the looks of these migrant worker-looking friends of yours, ugly is something they can't sidestep," Allen said sneeringly to Frankie.

"Wow, coming from a red-faced, leprechaun, alcoholic-looking motherfucker such as yourself, that shit is pretty funny," Frankie replied to Allen, both starting to show signs of aggression.

"Well, act like a tree frog and leap, bitch," Allen challenged Frankie.

"Everyone chill the fuck out," yelled Red, who began showing signs of nervousness when he realized that the situation was becoming erratic.

"Mmmmmmmmmm," Hynek painfully moaned. He grabbed his shoulder and saw the blood dripping off the palm of his hand, and yelled, "You're all dead!"

"What the fuck is his problem?" Allen sarcastically asked.

"Well, you did shoot the fucker," Red impudently replied. "Who is this fucking guy, anyway?"

"I don't know, this is the first time we've had any dealings with him," Sebastian explained, never losing eye contact with his childhood friend.

"Well, if he doesn't stop his fucking bitching right now, he's gonna get one right between his fucking eyes on his fucking fat, giant head," Allen agitatedly said.

"Take it easy, Al," Red attempted to calm him from his frustrated state.

"No, you take it easy. I'm done with all this bullshit," Allen replied.

"So, this is the company you're keeping with now?" Sebastian asked Red.

"Let me tell you a little something about company," Allen shouted as he aggressively pointed his pistol at Sebastian's head.

"Whoa, whoa, whoa!" Red yelled, hoping to stop Fabian and Frankie from shooting Allen. "

"Guys, it's late, we're all tired and extremely irritated from all this shit. Let's just put the guns down, come up with a solution and get the hell out of here before the cops get here. We're starting to get loud out here and all the gunfire is not helping."

"Fuck you, fuck this red-nosed Irish prick friend of yours and fuck this Russian fucker bleeding out."

"Frankie, take it easy," said Sebastian.

"Fuck that shit! Sean has been with us since we were all kids, helping each other no questions asked, and this is the respect we get from him?"

"Frankie—"

"No, Sebastian. Sean is here to turn us in like common criminals, and this obnoxious-looking fuck over here has been hired to take us out if we refuse to return—which, by the way, we're not going back."

"Now we're talking," Allen contentedly replied to Frankie.

"So, the choice is yours because I am tired of running away from all of this shit and I refuse to beg for mercy from these two assholes."

"So, now I'm an asshole? Before I was with you from the beginning," Red said to Frankie, who had his pistol pointed at Allen and was showing no signs of backing down.

"You've known us for a long time and you know we had nothing to do with what happened to that Jew fuck; and now you're here, so what the fuck does that say about you?"

"He's your boss too, Frankie."

"No, he's not, he's yours."

"Well, I don't give a fuck about your childhood, and I most certainly don't give a fuck about you. I was hired to bring all of you in and that's what I'm going to do," Allen angrily said to all of them as he pulled out a second pistol and pointed it at Red.

"Al, what the fuck are you doing?" Red asked, surprised by his partner's actions.

"Red, I'm starting to believe that you never had any intentions of bringing in your childhood amigos as ordered and I cannot have that," Allen replied with an impassive look.

"First of all, they're coming with me to see Avvi, dead or alive; and second, you better point that gun away from me or you are going to regret what you're doing real fucking fast," Red said to Allen with a demanding stare.

"Let explain something to you: You think this was Avvi's idea? Think again," Allen explained, catching Red by surprise.

"What the hell are you talking about?" Red asked with a distressed gaze.

"What, do you honestly believe you're the only one that was given the green light to move on and form a family? Well, guess again."

"Haha…" Hynek laughed with a condescending sneer. "No loyalty. That's why all of you today will die, and die by your own deception."

"Shut the fuck up, you stupid commie fuck," Allen yelled out as he kicked him in the face. He slightly lost his balance from the kick and saw Fabian attempt to go after him, but stopped him with a threat,

"Go ahead, you pretty motherfucker. You're the first one I'll shoot in the head."

"You know, now that I think about it, Avvi never mentioned you to me, or his approval of you," Red said to Allen, watching him look at Hynek flat on his back, semi-unconscious and feeling the pain from the kick.

"Fuck Avvi, he's just like you, a fucking nobody," Allen lashed out.

Bravado Brothers

"So, what? Are you gonna kill us all right here, right now?" Sebastian asked while looking at Red, who displayed a look of a man just betrayed.

"All of you just don't get it, do you? All of you fucked up and, at this point, are totally insignificant."

"Then I guess we're all going out blasting because there is no way I'm going with you back to Chicago," said Fabian, with his pistol aimed directly at Allen.

"Al, think about what you're about to do here," Red urged him. "It doesn't have to go down this way."

"All you had to do was play by the rules, Red, and none of this would have had to go down this way…oh well," Allen shrugged him off.

"Oh well," declared Frankie, closing one eye and focusing on his front sight.

For several imperceptible seconds, the unnerving silence screamed its declaration to seek ownership of the sinful souls that occupied the South St. Paul Rocky River banks. Sebastian, Fabian, Frankie, and Red, astounded by the stealthy cessation that temporarily rattled their receptiveness, remained motionless and watched in amazement as blood spurted out the exit wound between Allen's eyebrows.

Red, who was the closest one standing next to Allen and the first to receive the warm, foul-smelling splatter on his face, immediately realized that he was the next intended target to have his head blown off. He began to panic—the idea of being betrayed, turning his back on his childhood friends and prematurely leaving the earth did not settle well for him.

"What the fuck?" yelled Frankie as he watched Allen's face get blown off and his lifeless body land on the harsh terrain.

"Is everybody alright?" Sebastian shouted in question, wiping away the blood sprayed on his eyes.

"Who the fuck shot him?" Fabian asked, trying to make sense of what just happened.

"It was me, who wants to know?" Jardani said, walking toward them with his pistol drawn.

"Oh shit, I always knew I am a good shot, but did not realize I was that good," Jardani said in a praiseworthy manner to himself as he jauntily approached Allen's body to inspect his kill.

"What are you doing?" Tawno asked Jardani, who was taking a photo on his cell phone.

"Imagine me explaining this awesome kill shot to those ungrateful fucks at the Casino. They will never believe me," Jardani explained with a profound look. Tawno was still bothered by his actions.

"We need to get out of here right now," Tawno said to Jardani, ignoring Frankie, Fabian, Sebastian, and Red. "There have been a lot of shots fired here and I don't want to be anywhere around here when the police answer the call."

"But there are no homes around here—"

"I am growing tired of you disregarding everything I say," Tawno angrily replied, cutting off Jardani.

"Well, what are we gonna do about these assholes?" Jardani sarcastically asked as he realized pistols were being pointed at him and Tawno.

Tawno, who was psychologically and physically overwhelmed, sighed in frustration, realizing his troubles took a cliff dive for the worst.

"I do not know who all of you are, but my beef is only with him," Tawno explained, pointing to Red.

"Fuck him, take him with you," Frankie said, smiling at his childhood friend.

"Frankie, what the hell are you doing?" Fabian apprehensively asked.

"Yeah, what the fuck are you saying?" Sebastian joined in the questioning.

"In case you've forgotten, he isn't here because he wanted to catch up on old times," Frankie said, staring into Red's eyes.

"Good, I'm glad that this is settled because getting into a war over something as petty as a weakened friendship would be a bad thing for you all of you."

Sebastian and Fabian, who had known Frankie all their lives and understood that his level of reasoning is often best described as enigmatic, immediately identified his familiar exasperated gaze as he pointed his pistol at Tawno.

"No!" Sebastian yelled out from the top of his lungs. He shifted his aim at Jardani, who was now aiming his pistol at the back of Red's head.

"Is there a problem?" Tawno asked in confusion.

"As a matter of fact, there is," Frankie replied, and with that, he rapidly turned around and shot Jardani.

"You son of a bitch!" Tawno shouted. "We had an agreement."

"Yeah, I said take him with you, not shoot him."

"You motherfuckers," Tawno said to them as he knelt next to Jardani, placing a handkerchief over the gun wound to slow the bleeding. "You are all going to pay for this."

"No, we're not," said Khan. He and a small group of Vietnamese workers holding machetes and butcher knives silently approached the shoreline.

Fabian started chuckling at the sight of Khan and his entourage approaching them. He placed his hand over his mouth to cover his laughter and said to Khan, "You know, you're making this too easy for me."

Khan aggressively marched over to his brother and, standing directly in front of him, eye to eye, said, "When this is over, I am going to whip your ass for all the shit you've made us all go through out here."

Fabian saw the intensity in his brother's eyes and refused to reply; he knew Khan was like a ticking time bomb, ready to explode.

"Put your guns down, it's over for now," Khan ordered his brothers and Frankie, all of whom were ready to shoot.

"Screw you, Khan. The only things I'm putting down are these dog-looking fuckers over here, ready to shoot us," Frankie replied, never losing eye contact with Tawno and Jardani.

"I said, put them down. They're covered—anything goes down, they're the first to go."

"I hope you're right," Sebastian said to Khan, starting to feel fatigued, "Because I did not come all the way here just to get taken out by strangers."

"We are not here for you, we are here for him," Tawno said, referring to Red.

"I don't give a fuck what he's accused of, he is not going anywhere with you. As a matter of fact, all of you are coming with us," Khan ordered.

"Where are we going?" Sebastian asked.

"I'll explain everything when we're far away from here, but for now we need to leave. We just listened to the police band radio and soon enough they will figure out where all this gunfire is coming from," Khan explained.

"What about the Russian bear?" Sebastian asked as he placed his pistol away.

"We have no other choice but to bring him with us; besides, the tide is starting to rise," Khan said.

"We are not going anywhere with any of you. He needs help," Tawno argued, looking at Jardani who was starting to fade in and out of consciousness.

"We have a truck waiting for everyone. You want him to live, drag his ass in there," Khan sternly told him.

"No."

"Fine then, you take him to the hospital and you explain to them how he got shot, but we are out," Khan said to Tawno while Hynek was dragged out to the truck by Frankie and Fabian.

"I cannot drag him away like a dead carcass," Tawno angrily replied.

"Don't worry about that, we've got it," said Khan as he waved the Vietnamese workers over to aid in bringing Jardani to the delivery truck.

"Alright, before we go, you two fucks hand me your pistols," Frankie demanded of Red and Tawno. He also picked up Jardani's pistol laying several feet away from him and yanked Allen's out of his firm, dead grip.

As he gave a final visual sweep to ensure that his safety, as well Jardani's, was out of harm's way, Tawno spotted several vehicle lights from a distance, approaching from opposite directions. He felt unsettled, for he was unsure if those lights were friendly or hostile.

Tawno became even more distressed when he looked at Jardani, who had worked for him since he was a young boy. As he watched his faithful bodyguard be taken away and placed in the truck like frozen meat ready to be transported for delivery, Tawno vowed revenge.

Chapter XXI

Mistaken Identity

"Are we clear? ...Khan, are we clear? ...Khan!" Sebastian yelled.

"Yeah...yeah."

"What the hell was that all about?" Sebastian asked as he looked in the passenger side mirror at the headlights behind them.

"This is all fucked up. I mean, how did we even get to this point in our lives?" Khan asked in a stupefied manner.

"I don't know, but I did not get this far just to let it all slip away because of a misunderstanding. Fuck that and fuck 'em all," Sebastian replied. He turned toward the back seat and looked at Frankie, who sat next to Red, pointing his pistol at him. Sebastian said to Red,

"What I don't understand is why you didn't stick up for us, or even take the time to put the pieces together. I mean, fuck, Red—we were boys."

"You know it doesn't work that way," Red answered.

"Well, because of it not working that way, a lot of people died," Sebastian snapped. He faced forward again, stroking his hair in frustration as the car ride remained silent for a few seconds.

"What the fuck are you looking at, Frankie? You want to stop the car and you and I duke out?" Red angrily asked.

"Khan, stop the fucking car. I'm gonna kick this Irish motherfucker's ass," Frankie irately yelled. "I said stop the fucking car!"

"Calm the fuck down, you stupid fucks!" Sebastian shouted as he jumped between them, forcing Khan to swerve. He turned to Red and said,

"Let me tell you something, you stupid fuck: We have been there from the beginning. When Avvi needed something and didn't want to get his hands dirty, we were there. He has known us since we were all kids, and we were fucking loyal to that Jew fuck until he sent you and that stupid headless fuck to kill us."

"Avvi didn't send Allen," Red assured him.

"Who did then?" Khan asked. The whole car eagerly waited for an answer.

"You really don't know," Sebastian said, realizing Red had to think about the question.

"You guys need to understand that there are a lot of people involved in all this shit."

"Yet you don't know who's calling the shots," Sebastian pointed out to Red.

"Avvi is."

"Well, according to your dead friend who is being hacked to pieces right about now, he isn't; and it's pretty safe to assume that somebody will be eager to speak to him real soon," Khan commented as he turned to exit the main road.

"Who the fuck is behind us?" Sebastian asked. He realized the car behind them was mimicking their every move.

"I don't know, but rush hour traffic is starting to pick up, which doesn't help us," Khan uneasily replied.

"How long have you guys been out here?" asked Red.

"What the fuck, you writing a book?"

"Frankie, chill the fuck out."

"No, Sebastian, nothing has changed here—as a matter of fact, the minute I see something that isn't right, he's gonna get one in the fucking head."

"You know, Franco—"

"Don't call me Franco, you Irish red-faced fuck."

"You have a lot of anger built up in you, and I don't blame you. You're half Cuban, half Polish, which makes you a dumb spic."

"What the fuck are you laughing at?" Frankie said to Khan, who was laughing at Red's comment.

"Alright, this is the deal," Sebastian began explaining as Khan pulled in the back of the restaurant and saw that the delivery truck made it safely. "Frankie, you know I respect you and we wouldn't have made it this far had it not been for you, but you need to approach this with a level head."

Frankie, who realized he was on the verge of responding hastily, placed his pistol away, stared at Red one last time and exited the back of the car without saying a word. He knew their situation was far from being resolved.

Sebastian turned to Red and implored, "I know you're just doing what you have to do, but keep in mind that so are we. We had nothing to do with what took place at Avvi's, and for that very reason, we are all dealing with this nonsense."

"I don't know what to make of any of this bullshit right now," Red said with a skeptical look.

"Well, for the time being, shut the fuck up and let us deal with this shit because walking away from any of this is not going to happen at this second. We're gonna have to fix this Czech and gypsy bullshit, and I have a feeling that the headlights that were behind us are not friendly. And we, unlike you, are going to try to save your ass along with ours," Sebastian explained with a tiresome look.

"Believe me when I tell you that I am more than capable of getting myself out of this," Red said with a poised grin.

"I'm sure you can, however, this is our neighborhood, our rules," Sebastian reminded him, never revealing his disposition.

"Alright, Sebastian, you're the boss, I'll do it your way," Red agreed as he attempted to open the back door and smiled when he was unable to.

"I'm no boss, just looking out for the best interest of the crew."

"Boss or no boss, that right there is a major problem. I can assure you if this does not work out in your favor, shit's going to get ugly for all of us," Red said to him, pointing at Hynek being helped out the back of the truck.

"You're right, you're absolutely right," Sebastian replied with a deep sigh as he walked in the back door of the restaurant, and entered their office.

"Mr. Hynek, again, I do not know who you are or what is it you are asking of us, but whatever it is you feel has wrongly happened, I am sure it's all a misunderstanding," Sebastian explained as he sat on a small round table with Frankie and Fabian standing behind him.

"You obviously do not know who I am, and that lack of knowledge is going to cost you all dearly. I originally came to this shithole of a city to search for a few associates of mine; however, they are nowhere to be found and now I am dealing with you soon-to-be-dead assholes.

"Dead asshole, huh? Well, we'll see who will end up dead," Fabian challenged him.

Hynek crossly stared at Fabian, reading his every facial expression, then methodically stared at everyone who was in the room the same way.

"At first I said to myself, perhaps my associates were caught off-guard and fell victim to their enemies' cunningness; but now, after experiencing your work firsthand, there is no way you dumbasses are capable of achieving such a task."

Sebastian smirked at Hynek's offensive conjecture, leaned back in his seat, interlaced his fingers behind his head, inhaled deeply and closed his eyes.

"Well, I guess since us dumbasses, as you described, are incapable of performing such an undertaking, why are you here dealing with us in this shithole of a city?" Sebastian asked as he leaned forward and placed his arms on the table to address Hynek.

"Because the events that have taken place thus far do not allow me to dismiss that theory. As a matter of fact, with your obviously well-experienced resources—which, by the way, is ingenious—there is an outside possibility that all of you had something to do with their demise," Hynek animatedly explained.

"You sons of bitches better hope he makes it out alive because if he does not, this war is one you will not be lucky enough to walk away from," Tawno spat out as he was pushed into the room by Vietnamese workers.

"I forgot about this fucking guy," Fabian said to Frankie, who was eyeballing Red.

"Tawno, right?" Sebastian asked.

"Soon enough, when this is over, all of you will never forget my name," Tawno angrily said, staring at Red.

"Do you owe this guy money or something?" Sebastian asked Red.

"It's not worth explaining," Red replied as he eased back on the chair.

"Look, I don't know what the hell is going on here, but I am confident that I speak for most of us when I say that we don't know anyone here, nor am I aware that we owe anything to any of you," Sebastian explained to Hynek and Tawno.

"You know why I am here," Hynek said with an implacable gaze.

"Well, you keep mentioning some associates of yours; however, your associates are not here, nor do I know them," Sebastian explained, trying to sell his anecdote.

"Tell me where they are!" Hynek yelled as he gripped his aching body.

Fabian walked over to a wet bar directly behind Hynek and Tawno, poured some whiskey into separate glasses and served both of them. Sebastian glanced at Fabian, wordlessly reminding him the trouble he had caused by not properly disposing of the cell phones. He returned his gaze to Hynek, who picked up on the brothers' facial channel of communication.

"So, you do know where he is—good," said Hynek as he took a commanding swig of his drink. "Progress can certainly be beneficial for all of you."

"What does that mean?" Sebastian asked him.

"What it means is, that the sooner any of you ass-clowns tell me where my associates are, the more merciful I will become when I remove you from this world."

"Wow, that bullshit almost sounded as threatening as it was convincing," Frankie replied as he received a drink from Fabian.

"None of this matters," mentioned Tawno. "Soon enough this all going to come to a bad end for all of you."

"How so?" asked Frankie.

"You will all find out soon enough," Tawno began explaining, but stopped when four unfamiliar faces entered the room, silencing everyone occupying it.

The obvious leader of the group spoke up,

"Please, don't let my presence interrupt what you were about to say. It sounded pretty important, almost life-threatening, which will always capture the attention of any audience."

"And you are?" asked Tawno.

"Well, to you, I can assure you I am of no threat; however, to these men, I am very important—isn't that right boys?"

"Considering you are in my territory, I insist on knowing who you are," Tawno demanded. He smiled at the shocked look Sebastian, Fabian and Frankie displayed.

"My name is Myles, Myles Levine. I don't know what kind of strife these men have caused you, but rest assured they will no longer be of an inconvenience to you," said Myles as he walked over the wet bar and made himself a drink.

"So, you are now here to clean all this shit up?"

"Wait a minute, wait a minute—I told you my name but you didn't tell me yours," Myles interrupted him.

"Tawno Marks."

"Tawno Marks...are you like a gypsy or something?"

"Gypsy, you make it sound so bad. Almost as bad as being called a Jew," Tawno replied with an imprudent look in his eye.

Raspy laughter caught the attention of everyone who agreed or disagreed with Tawno's reply. Hynek, who remained seated in the corner of the room, nursing his body, looked at Myles, who was trying to keep his emotions in check.

"So, is this your help?" Myles asked Tawno.

"I do not know who he is, nor do I care."

"Oh, I see," Myles replied as he looked at Hynek's direction. "I'm sorry, we never formally introduced ourselves to one another," Myles respectfully addressed Hynek, approaching him and motioning to shake his hand.

"Damn, that motherfucker is laid out," one of Myles' associates uttered out. Myles had viciously struck Hynek with the side of his gun, sending him crashing to the floor.

"I hate being interrupted," Myles cynically remarked as he placed his gun in its holster and sat back down.

"Now, where were we?"

"So, tell me, why are you—" Tawno began asking.

"I am starting to lose my patience," Myles interrupted, pointing his finger up in the air. "Not to mention, this smelly looking manoosh here broke my concentration. You know what, now that I think about it, you're totally fucking irrelevant to any of this shit," Myles explained to Tawno. He turned to Fabian, Frankie, and Sebastian and said,

"There was a point, not long ago, where I believed I was never going to find any of you."

"Don't you turn your back to me," Tawno authoritatively commanded.

"What the fuck did you just say?" Myles yelled at Tawno, drawing his gun again and pointing it at his head, "Did I not just say I was losing my patience?"

He turned back to the group and continued, "Now, as I was saying before this inexcusable interruption, I truly believed I was never going to find any of you. However, here we are." He looked around the room and asked, "By the way, where is Allen? I don't recall seeing him. Also, where the fuck is that cock-toking cousin of mine?"

Sebastian immediately glanced at Red, who displayed a troubled blank look. He smiled as he reflected on the events that took place the day before with Ephraim, and just hours ago at South St. Paul.

"So, nobody wants to speak?" Myles asked, standing up from his chair. "I do know that my cousin was here because he reached out to me, telling me about you gonifs being here."

"So, you're the one that sent Allen to accompany me?" Red asked him, trying to puzzle the pieces together.

"Well, I knew that eventually you would find these numb-nuts here; however, I didn't trust you to return them back, so I sent Allen with you," Myles replied. "Am I off on that assumption?"

"I am loyal to your father," Red said to him.

"Perhaps, but we will never know."

"Did your father approve this?" Red asked.

"My father is home right now, recovering, so leave him out of this. Besides, he is about to step down and I will be taking over soon enough, so there you have it," replied Myles.

"So, what you're telling me is no, he does not?"

"You just don't get it, do you?" Myles shot back and confronted Red, toe to toe.

"Oh, I do—I do now."

"Good, so shut the fuck up."

"What the fuck are you looking at?" an associate of Myles said to Fabian, who was staring at him in a challenging manner.

"Motherfucker," said Fabian.

"What's up, Fabe?" Sebastian questioned.

"You're Stelios, aren't you? You were the intended target," said Fabian, smiling as he pointed at Myles' associate.

"What the fuck are you talking about, Fabe?" Red asked.

"That night in Chicago—you know, when we were all staking out who we thought was Stelios?"

"Is this the son of a bitch?" Frankie shouted as he pulled out his pistol, causing a chain reaction in the room.

"Whoa, whoa, whoa, now that's fucking intense," Myles yelled enthusiastically.

"We had to go into hiding because of you, you fucking son of a bitch!" Fabian screamed out in anger.

"Not my fault you shot the wrong man," Stelios replied as he aimed his gun intensely.

"Sebastian, who gave you the order?" Red asked.

"It was ordered from Avvi," Sebastian responded, trying to think back.

"So, you got that order directly from him?"

"No, he got it from me, and I got it from him," Khan intervened as he walked into the room, pointing at Myles.

"It was my understanding that Stelios was to go because he was heavily in debt with Antonio Mancini," Khan explained to Red. "But there was more to it, wasn't there?"

"You were humping on that Puerto Rican chick from the bar for some time," Red said to Stelios, who started showing signs of being nervous. "And Lorenzo, after losing all that weight, was humping on her as well, I remember him talking about it…Wait a minute, this was all about some girl?" Red asked, his eyes widening.

"You son of a bitch," said Fabian, staring down Myles. "You placed the order for us to purposely kill the wrong guy—which, by the way, we technically never killed him."

"Shut the fuck up, Fabe," Khan shouted in annoyance, hoping to ease the situation.

"Why? Why did you place such a deceptive order like that? She was just a skank that played all of you," Fabian angrily questioned.

"Because Myles and Stelios are fucking each other," Antonio Mancini assumingly shouted out as he walked into the room with Heiman Blasberg and two of his associates, whose guns were drawn.

Myles looked over at Stelios, revealing an intimate involvement. A firestorm of rage and confusion set off in the room.

"Wait a minute, wait a minute, I was just fucking around and put that out there so that we could all have a chuckle," Antonio Mancini explained. "You mean to tell me that you two shit extractors are really banging each other?"

"Oh, shit," gasped Khan in total amazement.

"So, let me get this straight: You had my son killed because you couldn't bear the thought of the truth being revealed that you two are fags and are blowing each other?" Antonio Mancini furiously shouted.

"Damn, I did not see that one coming," Sebastian remarked.

"This is why this world is going straight to hell, because of all the faggotry," Fabian added.

"This is a lot of fucking guns in one small room," Frankie laughingly observed. "All of this because of man ass."

"Fuck you, you spic motherfuckers," Myles yelled out in anger as he fired the first shot.

Tawno, who instinctively dropped to the floor and placed his arms over his head, screamed out in dismay as the hail of gunfire, brutal and unrelenting, grazed his body. Praying to God to spare his life, he looked across the room, underneath the table, and saw Hynek laid out on the floor, unresponsive. He accepted what he felt were his last moments on earth.

The gunfight lasted ten seconds, but felt like an eternity to Tawno. It ended with a deathly unnerving feeling that stiffened his body as he heard the random bodies drop to their demise.

The distinctive smell of firearms that saturated the air, along with the nauseating smell of blood, brought him back to when he was just a boy and his father would explain to him about the angel of death coming into the world to claim the souls of the wicked.

Visions of his father, followed by his wife, children and all those he loved raced through his mind. Tawno began to weep, for he believed that the angel of death's hunt of unworthy souls was upon him. Then, the eerie silence loomed in the atmosphere.

"Sebastian?" Red called out. The calm sound that death left in its wake made him hesitant to raise his head.

"I'm alright," Sebastian responded. "Khan, you alright?"

"Get the fuck off of me, Frankie," Khan yelled out.

"What's it feel like to have a real man on you?" Frankie jokingly responded as he rose to his feet. "Oh, shit," he said, his mood breaking as he saw Fabian lying on the floor with blood seeping through his back.

"Fabian!" Sebastian yelled out, terrified. He scanned the room for any movement posing a threat, and called out a second time, "Fabian, are you alright?"

"Frankie, help me look around and see whose still with us," Red said, staring at Sebastian and Khan who worriedly attended to their kid brother, Fabian.

"Mr. Mancini, are you alright?" Red asked, removing Mancini's associate off of him.

"Yeah, I'm alright…Fuck!" Antonio Mancini angrily replied as he looked at his bodyguard, who was shot in the back of the head.

"Do you hear that?" Red asked him. There was a faint sound of a body gasping for air.

"Well, look at what we have here," said Antonio Mancini, pointing to Myles.

"Whoa, what the fuck?" Antonio Mancini's second associate, who survived the onslaught, shouted. He swiftly moved to avoid being directly hit by the blood Myles was coughing out.

"You're a fucking piece of shit, and when I see you in hell, I will make you die over and over again," Antonio Mancini said to Myles, pointing his gun at him. "By the way, your little cock-toking boyfriend is dead with a fucking hole in his head—just thought you ought to know."

"Shit, the old Jew is still alive—took one in the shoulder, but still alive," yelled out Khan from across the room.

"Well, look at that, not all is lost. Now Heiman can tell your father how much of a…what the fuck do these gefilte fish-eating fucks call fags?" Antonio Mancini asked, snapping his fingers.

"Faygeleh," Khan responded.

"Yeah, that's it, a faygeleh," Antonio said to Myles. He squatted down so that he could antagonize him. "I get it, back in the day in ancient Greece, men banging other men was socially expectable—mainly because they were Godless people. However, a heb? Now that's fucked up. I mean, shit's just not looking good for you, is it?"

"Fuck you," Myles said to him with every little ounce of strength he could generate.

"No, Myles, fuck you!" Antonio responded. He screwed on his silencer and, in unison, Red, Antonio and his associate unloaded their magazines.

Antonio reloaded a fresh magazine and started walking toward Heiman. Cynically, he said, "Heiman, I have known you for a real long time and have made a lot of money with this family, but I am starting to wonder if you knew about all of this."

"No…"

"Come on, Heiman, say what's on your mind. In the end, you have an important decision to make here."

"I did not know," Heiman replied with a tearful look in his eyes.

"In all my years of being in this business, I really do not know what to do…I mean, I really do not know what to do. I lost a son—which, by the way, I did not forget about, you spic fucks," he yelled out. "I almost got shot and killed by Avvi's son—who, by the way, I have known since he was born and never, not once suspected him of being a semen-swallowing son of a bitch. And now, I've got a potential war between two families."

"Whoa, whoa, whoa," Red said loudly. He pointed his gun at Tawno, who finally had no other choice but to move.

"Now who the hell is that?" Antonio Mancini asked.

"His name is Tawno," Red replied with a smile.

"Tawno? What kind of a name is Tawno?"

"He's a gypsy," Red answered, shrugging his shoulders.

"Gypsy? What kind of Mickey Mouse operation are you guys running here? I'm gonna tell you something, this state is all fucked up," Antonio Mancini said, confused. "And who the hell is that bear-looking fuck over there, laid out?"

"Truthfully, we don't know who he is. He said his name is Hynek."

"Hynek? That sounds like a problem, Red," Antonio Mancini said, never paying attention to the direction of his gun, making Heiman uneasy.

"He's been laid out for some time."

"Is he dead?"

"No, but I'm sure he's going to be waking up real soon, in pain and ready to shoot someone," explained Red, staring at Hynek.

"Is he a problem? Do we need to take care of this nonsense right away?"

"Nah, we got him, Mr. Mancini. But, we have to make this quick—he doesn't know that you're here, which can be beneficial for you."

"Trust me, I'm not worried about him."

"Let's just be on the safe side, Mr. Mancini," Red explained to him, placing his gun inside its holster.

"Before you start with this awful-smelling cleanup here—and I don't think I need to stop and point out that there are a lot of bodies lying out here—what are we to do with my longtime Jewish friend, here?"

"Mr. Mancini, with all due respect, Heiman is good people. You know this, and I'm sure we can clear all this up, especially with Avvi."

"Yeah, something tells me Avvi is not going to take this well. Trust me, I know he's gonna want to respond, and rightfully so."

"I'll take care of that," Heiman interjected.

"And just like that, I'm supposed to walk away and not have to worry about any of this?"

"Mr. Mancini, I've been given the approval to start up," explained Red as he lifted Heiman to his feet.

"I heard—Chicago?"

"Haven't made that decision yet. Chicago is congested with a lot of our kind, and adding one more to that list isn't going to prove beneficial."

"No shit," Antonio Mancini replied, placing his gun in its holster.

"Then, you need to trust me about this," Red said to him with a steadfast demeanor.

"Let me tell you something, Red: In this business, trust is a misleading word. I tell you what, I'm gonna get the fuck out of here because I am too old for this shit, but I guarantee you that if this shit doesn't get fixed in every aspect, there is going to be a war you will not be able to get your Irish ass out of."

"Understood, Mr. Mancini," Red replied.

"And for you pieces of shit," Antonio Mancini addressed Sebastian, Khan, and Frankie. "I never want to see you near me again. As a matter of fact, I don't want to see you in Chicago ever again. Consider this a one-time consolation."

"Thank you, Mr. Mancini," Red said, speaking for his childhood friends and extending out a hand to Mancini.

"Forgive me, but right about now I am in no mood for shaking hands."

"Understood. What about your guy?" Red pointed to Mancini's dead associate.

"He was a street kid I was trying to bring in. Make sure you properly dispose of the body. Can you do that?"

"Yeah, I got it," Red replied, looking at Khan.

"Good. I am tired, in pain and I have a long drive home. I will see you in the much-later future," Antonio Mancini said to Red as he began walking out. Before leaving, he asked,

"So, is that pretty boy brother of yours going to make it?"

"I think so," Sebastian replied.

"Good, I've always liked him. It would have been a pity to have gotten rid of him, or all of you, for that matter."

"So, what are we going to do about them?" Frankie asked. They all looked at Hynek, who was still laid out, and Tawno, who looked perturbed.

"Today is your lucky day," Red sternly said to Tawno. "But, believe me when I tell you, not that lucky."

Chapter XXII

Goodbye For Now

"You look good, how are you feeling?" Red asked Fabian at an undisclosed location.

"I'm good. I've gotten a little sloppy, but that's what happens when you're laid up in bed for a long time," Fabian replied.

"You're good? What the hell are you talking about? You were being attended to, hand and foot, daily. Not to mention, getting a rim job just about every day from those women who can win a hotdog eating contest at Nathan's," Sebastian sarcastically commented.

"Damn, Fabe, you still like hogging it, I see," Red said with a chuckle.

"I can't help if they love me," replied Fabian as he finished packing and placed his suitcase near the door.

"So, where are you guys going?" Red asked. He knew it was going to be some time before he would see his best friends again.

"Well, I can't say much because I've never been, but I'm heading to Georgia with my lay friends. They have a lot of family out there, not to mention they just graduated from the university out there. I'll be in touch, don't worry," Fabian assured him.

"Are you heading with him?" Red asked Sebastian and Khan.

"For now, yes," Khan replied with a lot of skepticism.

"What the hell does that mean?" Red asked.

"He's just upset he isn't going to see that hot piece of ass back home for some time," Sebastian explained.

"Who, the girl at the hospital?"

Khan looked at Red to read his face for sincerity, and he saw right away that Red knew about her all along and was not going to question him.

"Come on, Khanee, did you really think she was going to be overlooked?" Red teased him. "Don't worry, she's good and I have a good feeling you'll be seeing her again real soon."

"You take care of yourself, Sean," Khan said with a sad face and a big hug, followed Fabian, who could not look at Red straight in the eyes.

"It's for the best. Besides, I'm going to be a boss now and will have a say-so on a lot of things, including you dumb fucks," Red replied.

"Take care, Red."

"The two of you be good," Red said to Fabian and Khan.

Khan walked out the door and turned to Sebastian, who was lingering inside. "Sebastian, we gotta hit the road soon, this is one long trip," he reminded him.

"I'll be right there," Sebastian replied, placing the final suitcase near the door. He requested to Red, "Listen, tell Frankie I'm sorry for not saying goodbye to him."

"Sebastian, he's in Massachusetts right now, getting things up and running for me. Besides, it's not like you're never going to see him again."

"I know, but that man has gotten us out of a lot of trouble. It is, after all, why we're still alive."

"I understand, but believe me when I tell you he's got nothing to worry about and neither do you."

"What, his cousin Adam?"

"I also gave him a job. I hope he works out."

"Nah, he's a good kid. He'll do well."

"Good."

"So, Massachusetts, huh?" Sebastian asked as he walked out the door.

"Yeah, I have a perfect location. Don't worry, we'll stay in touch. It just has to be this way for now."

"I know. Well, I guess this is it for now."

"For now, Sebastian."

"Take care of yourself," the two said to one another as they began walking toward their vehicles.

"Hey, by the way, whatever happened to that gypsy guy and Boris, or whatever his name was?" Red asked before he entered his car.

"We dropped them off safely in Superior, Wisconsin. Trust me when I tell you, that is all you're gonna want to know," Sebastian said with a smile.

"That'll work," replied Red with a grin.

It is with great joy, and sincere gratefulness that my Lord, and heavenly maker has bestowed upon me the ability and the gift to transcribe into literary life, the never ending cinematic stories and anecdotes continuously played in my head.

Finding my true calling was more than an accomplishment for me, it became a spiritual awakening. I now understand, feel, and live.

I am completed and balanced as an individual by my children, my soulmate, and most importantly, GOD's Grace.

I was born and bred in Brooklyn, New York, and I currently live in Jackson County, GA. I am currently working on my latest novel that is on track to be completed and released; God willing, by late 2018.

To second chances and boundless opportunities….Salute!

-Ildefonso

ildefonso@nyrpublishing.com

Made in the USA
Coppell, TX
14 November 2021